Irish Log

IRISH LEGAL ANECDOTES

Joseph McArdle

GILL & MACMILLAN

Gill & Macmillan Ltd
Goldenbridge
Dublin 8
with associated companies throughout the world
Joseph McArdle 1995
0 7171 2137 2

Design and print origination by
O'K Graphic Design, Dublin

Printed by
ColourBooks Ltd, Dublin

A catalogue record is available for this book from the British Library.

1 3 5 4 2

CONTENTS

For thirty-one years there were Assizes at Belcarra and for fifty years they were held there and in Ballinrobe alternately.

Criminals condemned to death in Belcarra were executed from a tree on the lands of the neighbouring Abbey of Ballintober. Hence the ditty:

Shake hands, brother—you're a rogue and I'm another; You'll be hanged at Ballinrobe and I'll be hanged at Ballintober.

INTRODUCTION

Shay and Barry, an architect and a solicitor, decided to visit their college pal, Peter, who was farming in the west of Ireland. They were all fishermen and, on the second day, they went out on Lough Conn but the fish did not bite. So they talked about their lives since college and somehow found themselves wondering who belonged to the oldest profession.

'No problem,' said Peter. 'Adam was a gardener and even when he was expelled he had to earn his bread by the sweat of his brow in the field. Farming is the oldest profession.'

'Hold on,' Shay protested. 'If you want to bring the bible into it, go back to the very beginning of *Genesis*. God made order out of chaos. God is the great architect. Sorry, mate, we were here before you.'

Barry was silent and they turned towards him expectantly. He thought for a moment. 'But who made chaos?' he asked.

Anyone trapped in a long lawsuit might well agree with Barry, and the average citizen regards a visit to a solicitor's office as considerably lower down the list of pleasurable experiences than a trip to the dentist. This is why we have lawyer jokes. 'How do you know whether it's a squashed hedgehog or a lawyer on the motorway?' 'If there are skid marks, it's a hedgehog.' 'Why do you never see a lawyer with his hands in his pockets?' 'Because they're always in somebody else's.' A man, who asked for advice from his solicitor in Ballinasloe, was told that on the one hand he could do this and on the other hand he could do that.

When the solicitor then asked him what he wanted, he replied, 'A one-handed solicitor'.

Views differ, of course. Jack Cade said, 'First, let's kill all the lawyers,' but Daniel O'Connell described the Irish bar as 'the first profession in the world—the only profession, with the single exception perhaps of the military, to which a high-minded gentleman would condescend to belong.' While it may seem to the woman on the Tallaght bus that lawyers create chaos, the alternative to civic chaos is law and order; the alternatives to the pompous rituals, the theatricality, the delays and frustrations are vigilantes, lynch law and the rule of thugs. Which does not mean that law and justice are identical!

A book of legal anecdotes, offered as a relaxation and an entertainment, becomes, in spite of itself, a mini social history of Ireland from the late eighteenth century to the present day. Jonah Barrington portrays the world of the Anglican ascendancy bucks, Yeats's indomitable Irishry; Richard Lalor Sheil is polemical in support of the emerging Roman Catholic gentry, with a backward look to the 'old English landowners'; Serjeant Sullivan and his nephew Maurice Healy link Victorian Ireland and the twentieth century and highlight the close bonds between judicial careers and the fortunes of the Tories and Liberals across the water. A book of legal anecdotes mirrors the divide between city and country and the descending importance of land, money, religion and sex in Irish lives.

Above all, this book seems to reply to Pilate's question, 'What is truth?' with the answer that in an Irish court truth is relative and that, many years ago, the Irish country woman and man grasped the essence of the common law which still baffles learned continental jurists. The function of the court in an adversarial system is not to arrive at the truth but to attempt, with varying degrees of success, to ensure some element of fair play in a highly artificial competition.

Barristers have been compared to actors and there is truth in the comparison. But a less frequent comparison is equally valid, that with prize-fighters. Every case is a contest. The outcome is never certain. The consequent stress and anxiety of preparation, of mastering details and marshalling facts, which must be on the tip of counsel's tongue when he is on his feet before a critical audience, should give more reason for stage-fright and fast-flowing adrenalin than the repetition of a part which has been rehearsed and played a score of times before. So the Bar seeks release from tension. In Inns of Court and on circuit, their hobby-horses are vinous and anecdotal and the passage of Medoc and port is a great encouragement to talk shop. There are no better talkers of shop in the world. I once spent my holidays in a picturesque village in Umbria, a world away from the Law Library. We were invaded by a brief of barristers and for a week, olive trees, poplars and medieval *castellos* disappeared and, like the House of Loreto, the *fattoria* was miraculously translated to the banks of the Liffey.

There is no end to stories about the law and lawyers, most of them told by lawyers themselves. They have always been their own publicists. They also write memoirs. Distractions were few down the country before the arrival of the kinematograph, not to mention television, and mess dinners were prolific breeding grounds of anecdotes which moved out like viruses among the healthy population and multiplied. The problems of compiling a book of legal anecdotes do not arise therefore from lack of material but from the need to select and exclude.

It will be seen that in the process of selection five main themes have emerged. Internal and external sparring: the interplay of wit and point-scoring between judges and barristers, barristers and solicitors, all three and witnesses and juries. Social history: Irish attitudes over the centuries to honour, sex, alcohol, inheritance, entertainment and position in society and the ivory tower which the profession has built around itself. Religion: the exclusive right of members of the Church of Ireland to higher legal office, the creation of West Britons by 'the admission of professional and genteel Catholics to Parliament and to the honours of the professions', Roman triumphalism. Politics: the symbiotic closeness of law and politics in the old Irish House of Commons, in Westminster and in Dáil Eireann. Language: the marvellous flights of rhetoric and word-play from the bench, the bar and the dock and the equally felicitous description of these *dramatis personae* by diarists and memoir-writers.

A description of two Irish judges: 'Each of them was bathed in the waters of the common law, and looked upon statutory enactments as a bather might consider the limitations of his pool, or the dam that contained his waters.'

A condemnation of a litigious family: 'The Duffy family was very sickly; it was also rather fraudulent. The illnesses from which its members suffered in turn gave the convalescents opportunities to try to overreach the invalids.'

A euphemism for mistresses: 'Those moveable objects of unwedded endearment, which Lord Thurlow used to recommend to the juvenile members of the profession.'

If all the above sounds very serious, this is because it is a bare-faced attempt to give spurious status to a light-hearted romp through two centuries of forensic tomfoolery.

Enjoy.

ABUSE

Lawyers and those connected in any way with the law have never been slow to indulge in healthy abuse.

Blaise Luttrel was an unlikeable barrister, a bully and a snob. His income came mainly from Workmen's Compensation cases where he appeared for insurance companies. Quarrelsome in drink, he was once barred from the barristers' regular haunt in a town in the south of Ireland but, a close friend, an English insurance salesman, stuck by him and continued to drink with him in a nearby pub until he had purged his contempt. Shortly after his return to the fold, he brought up the subject of his faithful pal.

'Take Formby now,' he said, 'he's a decent enough chap. Got a good head on him but, you know, he's not what I would call a gentleman.'

Only one of his companions could find words to express their common reaction. 'And three times the cock crew,' he remarked drily.

Somebody asked Richard Lalor Shiel once to define 'gravity' and he replied, 'Leslie Foster. He advances to his seat at the inner bar, like a priest walking in a procession. He lays down his bag on the green table, as if he were depositing a treasure. He bows to the court like a mandarin before the Emperor of China, quotes Tidd's *Practice* as a Rabbi would read the Talmud, and opens "The Rules and Orders" as a sorcerer would unclasp a book of

1

incantation. That is gravity.'

Foster became a puisne Baron of the Exchequer, and one comment on his performance there was that 'a man may be solemn without being wise, and circumstantial without being accurate,' but the final word goes to Chief Baron O'Grady. In his old age, he retired to his country seat to enjoy his last days. Someone in the house had a pet owl whose cage was in the old Chief's favourite room. He endured it for some time, but at length became uneasy and called out to one of his family, 'Take away that owl. He reminds me of Leslie Foster.'

———————

Lord Manners, on his retirement, was awarded £200,000 of public money for his 'distinguished ability, strict impartiality and unremitting assiduity'. He used his farewell address to launch an attack on the newly appointed Solicitor General, a Mr Doherty.

This was the subject of discussion some months later between members of the bar.

'You are surprised at Manners' attack on the Solicitor General?' one asked the other.

'I am not surprised that he gave vent to his factious antipathies to Mr Doherty. He was motivated by political rancour owing to Doherty's support for Catholic Emancipation. No, I am not surprised. What does make me wonder are the ostensible grounds that Manners earlier advanced when opposing Doherty's appointment: lack of seniority and the exercise of parliamentary or political interest.'

'These seem fair grounds for objection.'

'Objections to the head of his circuit from a man who had been unemployed at the English bar, except when he got a brief from his brother-in-law, a solicitor of Lincoln's Inn?'

'But political patronage?'

'Only the fact that he was the uncle of the Duke of Rutland and the brother of the Archbishop of Canterbury could ever have raised a man of Manners's feeble understanding and slight acquirements to the office of Lord Chancellor of Ireland, to the discharge of whose duties he was so utterly incompetent that Lord Hart, his able and erudite successsor, can scarcely refrain from expressing astonishment at the spirit of blunder in which almost every one of Lord Manners's orders, which come before him for revision, is conceived.'

A comedy of Manners, indeed.

Con Molloy, the leader of the Connaught Circuit, punctuated his speech with ejaculation of the phrase 'into it' prefaced by a grunt. 'May it please your Lordships,' he would say, 'I appear—huh—into it—with my friend Mr Brady on motion—huh—into it—to make absolute—huh—into it—a conditional order.'

Next to Con in the old Law Library sat Hyacinth Plunkett. He had a slight limp. Con and Hysie were lifelong friends and had gone through the world without a shadow of difference until one day Hysie was called to the door and on his return Con said, 'D'ye know, Hysie—huh—into it—I've been sitting here beside you for twenty-two—huh—into it—years, and I never noticed before that—huh—into it—you've got a kind of a string halt in your walk.'

Hysie lifted his shrill falsetto voice. 'And if you had manners, Con,' he trilled, 'you'd have been twice as long and you never would have remarked it. I've been sitting next to you for twenty-two years and I never remarked that you'd a kind of a string halt in your speech.'

How would the Ceann Comhairle today react to Grattan's reply to an accusation that it was his (Grattan's) advice which had brought about the rebellion of 1798?

Had any men out of the House said what the honourable gentleman has said in the House, my answer would have been a blow. I care not how high

3

his situation, how frivolous his character, whether he is a privy councillor or a parasite, a half coxcomb or a half swindler, my answer would be a blow.'

And a blow would naturally be followed by pistols for two.

———————

Before a certain judge was raised to the Irish bench, he had been known as Counsellor Necessity, because 'Necessity knows no law.' It was later remarked of him that he 'consistently merited the cognomen after his elevation as well as before'.

———————

An extract from a newspaper profile of a judge, one hundred years ago:

There is not a journalist in the country who has anything to learn from the impudent little man in horse-hair, a microcosm of conceit and empty-headedness . . . One is almost sorry that the Lord Chancellor had not another relative to provide for on the day that he selected a new judge from among the larrikins of the law. One of the judge's biographers states that 'an eccentric relative left him much money.' That misguided testator spoiled a successful bus conductor.

———————

Two barristers were talking about another who had moved to the English bar. 'I don't think he'll set the Thames on fire,' said one. 'No, not unless he's insured it first,' replied the other.

———————

Lord Morris and Killanin had the tongue of a Thersites which he could use to good effect. Heartily wishing a plague on both of them, he christened the two nationalist camps after the Parnell split, the 'Shealyites' and the 'Healyites'.

Morris was a loyal unionist who, nevertheless, recognised the basic illogicality and impracticality of the English attempt to rule Ireland, for it was he who explained that 'the difficulty [in Anglo-Irish relations] lies in a slow-witted race trying to govern a quick-witted one.'

On another occasion, Morris was driven by exasperation to exclaim, 'I've known twenty-six Chief Secretaries for Ireland in my time, and I declare to God there is not one of them who, after he has been in Ireland three days, would not undertake to show me the way up my own backstairs.'

Daniel O'Connell's description of an address by Attorney General Saurin is as fine a piece of abuse as one can find:

A farrago of helpless absurdity, violent and virulent, it was a confused and disjointed tissue of bigotry, amalgamated with congenital vulgarity. He called my client a malefactor, a Jacobin and a ruffian. He called him a brothel-keeper, a pander, a kind of bawd in breeches. I cannot repress my astonishment that the Attorney General could have preserved this diet in its native purity; he has for some years mixed among the highest orders in the State; he has the honour to belong for thirty years to the first profession in the world—to the only profession, with the single exception perhaps of the military, to which a high-minded gentleman would condescend to belong—the Irish bar. With this galaxy of glory flinging their light around him, how can he alone have remained in darkness? How has it happened that the twilight murkiness of his soul has not been illuminated with a single ray shot from their lustre? How can he have memory enough to preserve his original vulgarity? From my inmost soul I bestow upon him my compassion and my boundless pity.

BAR AND BENCH

Judges are umpires, and barristers and solicitors are players. In the game which is the Common Law adversarial system, they need one another, but conflicts inevitably arise.

Shortly after John Philpot Curran had been called to the bar in 1775, he crossed swords with one Judge Robinson. Robinson was notorious as having been the author of 'many scurrilous and anonymous political pamphlets' which earned him his promotion to the bench. Some pronouncement by the judge provoked the fledgling barrister to say that he had never met the law, as laid down by his Lordship, in any book in his library.

'That may be, sir,' said the judge, 'but I suspect your library is very small.'

Curran replied: 'I find it more instructive, my Lord, to study good works than to compose bad ones. My books may be few but the title pages give the writers' names and my shelf is not disgraced by any such rank absurdities that their authors are afraid to own them.'

'Sir,' thundered Robinson, 'you are forgetting the respect that you owe to the dignity of the judicial character.'

'Dignity, is it!' retorted the young barrister. 'My Lord, on that point may I cite you a case from a book of some authority with which I have no doubt your Lordship is familiar.'

He then briefly related an incident from the novel *Roderick Random* by Smollett in which a character called Strap who, having stripped off his coat to fight, gave it to a bystander, but when the fight was over, found there was no coat and no bystander.

'So, my Lord,' he ended, 'when the person entrusted with the dignity of the judgement seat lays it aside for a moment to enter into a disgraceful personal contest, it is in vain when he has been worsted in an encounter that he seeks to resume it—it is in vain that he tries to shelter himself behind an authority that he has abandoned.'

Robinson sheltered instead behind the familiar threat of cornered judges: 'Sir, if you say another word, I'll commit you.'

To which Curran replied: 'If your Lordship does so, we shall both have the consolation of reflecting that I am not the worst thing your Lordship has committed!'

The notorious Lord Clare hated John Philpot Curran. When he was Attorney General Fitzgibbon, Curran accused him of sleeping when statutes of a most cruel kind were being enacted and ironically lamented that the slumber of guilt should so nearly resemble the repose of innocence.

They fought a duel over this and later when Clare went to the bench, he did everything he could to ruin Curran. Whenever Curran appeared in his court, he interrupted him, harassed him, made fun of him so that Curran lost a lot of clients and business.

Clare did not, however, always get his own way. Once, when he knew that Curran would be appearing before him with a very elaborate argument, he brought a Newfoundland dog into court with him and sat it up on the bench beside him. As the case went on, he seemed to pay more attention to the dog than to Curran. At the vital part of Curran's argument, he stooped down to fondle the dog and Curran stopped in mid-sentence.

'Go on, go on, Mr Curran,' said the Lord Chancellor, waving his hand at Curran but still looking at the dog.

'I beg a thousand pardons, my Lord,' said Curran, 'I

really took it for granted that your Lordship was employed in consultation.'

There was once a barrister who believed that judges should be impartial and that it should be of no concern to them whether a man was convicted or acquitted. After a hard day in court, he was thoroughly fed up with a judge who had insisted on ramming his opinion on the facts down the jury's collective throat and had made sure that his client was convicted. Afterwards, the registrar commiserated with him but the barrister would not be consoled.

'It's all your fault,' he replied. 'You put the wrong bloody question to the foreman of the jury. You should have asked him if they had found for his Lordship or against him.'

Many barristers feel that they know more law than the old man on the bench and some of them are not afraid to show it. Serjeant Sullivan, when asked by a very irritating judge what his authority for his absurd proposition was, turned to his junior and said, 'Hand me up the Sale of Goods Act, so that I can remind myself of it and introduce his Lordship to it.'

Serjeant Sullivan was once appearing before Lord Glenavy, the Lord Chancellor. Glenavy obviously favoured Sullivan's opponent and kept interrupting the Serjeant and breaking up the flow of his argument. Sullivan, however, paid no attention and kept going, hammering home point after point. He mentioned a particular bit of evidence which had been discussed already.

The Lord Chancellor saw an opening.

'Serjeant, doesn't that confirm the suggestion I was putting to you a few moments ago?'

'My Lord,' said Sullivan suavely, 'everything is confirmatory of a prejudice.'

In 1912 in Tralee, Sullivan was appearing before a man who was not merely an inadequate judge but also a deaf one. An old woman witness said to the judge, 'Me Lord, ye'll have to shpake up to me, for I'm very old and I'm very deaf.'

'And if you're only very stupid too,' said Sullivan, in a voice loud enough to be heard by everyone except the judge, 'you're well qualified to give evidence in this court.'

Serjeant Sullivan was pursuing a legal argument in the appeal against the conviction of Roger Casement. One of the judges in Casement's trial before a jury, Lord Avory, had defended an Irishman named Lynch against a charge of treason in the Boer War. He had raised the same point that Sullivan was raising, but it had been snuffed out by the Court on the authority of two cases cited by Coke three hundred years previously.

Sullivan demonstrated to the satisfaction of the court that neither of these cases of Coke's had anything to say to the point at issue and he was proceeding to criticise other citations of the seventeenth-century jurist, when Darling J. inquired, 'Are you saying, Serjeant Sullivan, that Lord Coke was always wrong?'

Sullivan replied, 'My Lord, it is as impossible for a judge to be always wrong as it is for him to be always right.'

'Yes,' said Darling, 'some of us have found that out for ourselves.'

A barrister, who had no time for lesser legal brains even when covered by a bob-wig, was never afraid to hit back if he felt that the judge was being a nuisance, so much so that one of his victims pulled rank one morning.

'Misther Ronan, Misther Ronan, you forget yourself!' said the judge. 'You lay down the law, as though it were your province to do so; please remember that in this court it is I who lay down the law.'

Ronan was having none of it. 'Your Lordship,' he reminded the judge, 'will please remember that I am here to teach you the law, so that, if possible, you may lay it down correctly.'

Coming out of court one day, a barrister had a very long face. A colleague who had had to go into another court, came up to him.

'Well, what was the judgement like?'

'I declare to God, Mick,' he said, 'it was like a pig with the shits—a little here, a little there, and nothing substantial anywhere.'

Once a barrister called William Johnson was pressing Judge Tom Kelly very fiercely to a decision in his favour, and stating as an argument, in his usual peremptory tone to judges he was not afraid of, that there could be no doubt on the point—precedent was imperative in the matter since his Lordship had decided the same points the same way twice before.

'So, Mr Johnson,' said the judge looking archly, shifting his seat somewhat, and shrugging up his right shoulder, 'so, because I decided wrong twice, Mr Johnson, you'd have me do so a third time? No, no, Mr Johnson, you must excuse me. I'll decide the other way this bout.'

Chief Baron Palles was another judge who was not ashamed to change his mind. He once made an order adverse to a defendant's junior counsel in the absence of his senior. When the senior came into the court, he arrived to hear the Chief Baron discussing the form of the order to be made against him. He protested against the proceedings and pointed out an error in a vital document before the court. The original was sent for and the error rectified. Palles then called on counsel for the plaintiff to deal with this new point.

The latter was upset by this and protested.

'Twenty minutes ago,' he argued, 'the Court expressed the opinion that I was entitled to carry my motion.'

'Speaking for myself,' said the Chief Baron, 'I confess that I was foolish enough to make some observations to that effect, but you can learn a lot in twenty minutes, my young friend, if you will listen.'

In a complicated case before Chief Baron Palles, a leader was being upstaged by his junior, Tom Bodkin. At the closing of the evidence, he had his revenge on Bodkin. He turned to him and said, 'Tom, you will now address the court.' At that time, Bodkin's practice was not big enough to put any great strain on him and he had had plenty of time to make up his brief. As a result, he spoke for about an hour.

Now, Palles was not a silent judge. He liked to participate fully in every case, i.e. he interrupted frequently and argued and questioned (although, in fairness to him, he never closed his mind until the last word had been said). On this occasion, he said nothing for the first twenty minutes but followed closely what Bodkin had to say, nodding occasionally in agreement or shaking his head. During the next twenty minutes he intervened with a good many questions and comments, all of them relevant and helpful.

When Bodkin sat down, the Chief Baron slapped his desk emphatically, kicked the front of the bench (normal practice for him when mildly excited), leant over and tapped the wig of his clerk, Frank Kennedy, who sat below him. As Frank Kennedy rose and turned to him, Palles exclaimed, almost petulantly, in ringing tones which could be heard throughout the court, 'See, see, Frank, you were entirely wrong. He made an excellent speech.'

Frank Kennedy, a kindly man, had warned him that Bodkin was inexperienced and might be easily put off by too frequent judicial interruptions, and Palles, having curbed himself during the first part of the address, felt somewhat aggrieved but nevertheless held for the plaintiff.

Traditionally barristers in the middle of the nineteenth century robed at home and walked to the courts with their brief-bags slung on their shoulders. At the midday interval the hungry advocates stood or walked around the central hall consuming refreshments, and a considerable amount of stale bun crumbs as well as orange and apple peel were to be found in the recesses behind the statues, when the hall emptied and the courts ceased their labours.

The great leaders of the bar drove to their work in those days and brought with them their 'body servants' or valets, who had mysterious ways of preparing light meals on trays. Later the advent of the thermos flask and the spaciousness of the new library gave a new life to the system of the home-provided snack until the habits of the professional class turned to heavier midday meals. The judges always had their meals in their chambers.

The last survivor of the old school of counsel was a man called MacDonagh, who persisted in robing at home and driving down, accompanied by his valet and his luncheon basket. MacDonagh always wore white gloves as part of his professional costume. He was a man in the front rank of the pettifogging system of demurrer that was successfully abolished in Ireland by the Judicature Act of 1877. He ended his career ingloriously as the successful defendant in an action brought to recover a special fee which he had taken to go down to a case at assizes. He had remained in town to attend to other cases, but had kept the fee, which ethically he should have returned. The client had no legal redress and MacDonagh died before the Benchers could deal with him.

MacDonagh's refreshment, like his refreshers, was on a generous scale, and he always pressed the judges for a long adjournment for lunch. Warren, president of the Probate and Matrimonial Division, was a bad-tempered dyspeptic who could not enjoy his own lunch and was not inclined to make things sweet for a counsel whom he bitterly disliked. In the middle of a probate case, when a glass of sherry and a plate of biscuits appeared on the bench, MacDonagh suggested that it was time to adjourn for lunch.

'I am not going to adjourn for lunch,' snapped Warren.

'At all?' inquired MacDonagh.

'At all.'

MacDonagh signalled for his valet, Charles, issued some orders and went on with the case. Warren munched a biscuit and sipped his sherry. Presently in came Charles, who cleared a space on the table in front of MacDonagh, put down a cloth and duly arranged silver, cutlery and glass. Warren glared at him. The next development was the entry of Charles with a tray on which was a plate containing a roast partridge and two small silver dishes of vegetables. The final blow to Warren was the unmistakable explosion of the cork issuing from a champagne bottle, but the sour-faced judge was afraid of the advocate and said nothing.

MacDonagh took his time to his meal, cross-examining witnesses with a fork in his hand, or arguing a point of evidence between sips of champagne. It was the only performance of his that was remembered with sympathy by the profession.

———————

There was once a squabble over the division of the assets of a deceased testator, whose will was somewhat ambiguous. Counsel for the plaintiff was Paddy Flemming, who was notorious for expressing simple matters in a manner comprehensible to himself alone.

''Tis how the testator, my Lord, was an old man who died a bachelor at the end of his life, unmarried, leaving no widow or children him surviving.'

'God blesh me sowl,' said Charlie Barry LJ, who spoke with a whistle through a broken tooth. 'What an egshtraordinary shtate of shircumshtances.'

———————

The more one reads of the history of the courts and the misbehaviour of bench, bar and witnesses, the more one is inclined to agree with the announcement made by Judge William O'Brien one day at the Cork Winter Assizes. The antecedents of a convicted prisoner were being discussed.

'Can you tell me anything about him?' O'Brien asked his counsel.

'As far as we know, my Lord, he is a travelling conjurer going about to fairs—a sort of mountebank.'

'A mountebank, Mr Adams? Do you tell me so! And what is he doing here? There are no vacancies in this court.'

Sir John Chute Neligan had served on the bench in other areas before becoming the recorder of Cork towards the end of the last century, and had a habit of invoking his former experiences whenever something new or startling swam into his ken.

'God bless my soul,' he would exclaim, 'I have presided over the court in nine different counties, but I never heard of anything to equal this.'

Naturally, he became known as Neligan of the Nine Counties and was quite pleased with the nickname.

As he grew older he became increasingly deaf, but it was judicious deafness. It is true that there were times when he could not hear, but there were also occasions on which he would not hear. Two solicitors in his court had an uncontrollable, albeit unconscious, habit of swearing. The first solicitor, whenever a client offered some particularly damning evidence against his client, would sniff twice and mutter, 'Holy God, did you hear that shite?' If the same thing happened to the second solicitor, he would utter a drumming sound and exclaim, 'Jesus Christ, what frigging perjury!' Neligan never heard a word.

If other solicitors overstepped the mark consciously, his hearing was acute. Once two young solicitors lost their tempers with each other and, out of the sides of their mouths, abused each other in whispers in the body of the court. Neligan leant forward and spoke as clearly as only the deaf can.

'The statute,' he pronounced, 'has appointed me to be a judge of law and equity within certain limits; but when two of the officers of my court introduce a controversy as to which is the biggest ass, I must ask them to refer me to the section that gives me jurisdiction to decide that.'

Two noted barristers, Chris Micks and Fitzgerald Kenny, suffered from Roy Jenkins' inability to make a distinction in pronunciation between 'r' and 'w'. One day they were both in a case involving some very belligerent travellers in Spiddal. Fitzgerald began by setting out the background for the judge.

'M'Lud, on the fifth of Apwil they wowed in Wowy Wafferty's licensed pwemises.'

Incomprehension furrowed the judge's brow.

'They wooed, Mr Fitzgerald Kenny? Is this a sexual case? A village wooing, ha, ha.'

'Oh no, m'Lud, it was a wow not a wooing, a weally bad wow.'

'I've never come across a wow before. Is it an animal?'

Chris Micks came to the rescue. 'Not at all, m'Lud, he is talking about a wegular wow, almost a wiot. You know the sort of thing, a wumpus.'

A barrister named Devlin, who was a double for Billy Bunter, had more tricks up his sleeve than a conjurer. His ultimate weapon was collapse and pained innocence. On one occasion, he did not appear when his case was called and only waddled panting into court, sweating and worried, when the list was almost over.

'Where were you, Mr Devlin?' asked the judge, annoyed at the disruption of the order of events. 'Why weren't you here when your case was called?'

'Ah, don't put that question to me, me Lord,' pleaded Devlin Bunterishly, 'not that question.'

'What other question should I put? I want to know where you were.'

'You don't want to know, me Lord.'

'But I do want to know, Mr Devlin.'

'Ah, me Lord, if I told you what I was up to now, it would only make it worse.'

Barney Shillman had written the standard work on Workmen's Compensation and, in consequence, received a lot of work in that area. He knew his subject inside out and had little time for the courtroom flourishes and suavity of the old Clongownians or St Columban's.

He was appearing for an injured workman once before the strait-laced Chief Justice Sullivan. A condition of a successful claim was that the workman should have notified a relevant person about the accident. This he had failed to do. Barney was arguing that the employer knew all about the accident so there was no need to tell him. The employer was contesting that no accident had occurred.

The Chief Justice, who was notoriously polite and patient, listened to Shillman for a long time but finally cut across him.

'Mr Shillman, I hear everything you say and it is most valuable but, in the end of the day, is it not a fact that your client failed to notify this accident?'

'You could say that, my Lord, yes, you could.'

'And when I say failed to notify, I mean that he told nobody about it, not his wife. Don't you find that a little hard to swallow?'

'Ah now, my Lord, we wouldn't have much of a life if we told our wives everything, would we?'

Barney lost his case.

Lord Mayne often sat on the bench with Lord Norbury, who was a buffoon. The total opposite of Norbury, Mayne was a man who illustrated to perfection La Rochefoucauld's maxim that 'gravity is a mystery of the body to hide the defects of the mind.' The profound calm of his imperturbable face and the continuous nodding of his head made him seem to his colleagues like the figure of Confucius which used to be plastered on the dome of the Four Courts. His long and measured sentences issuing in tones of oracular wisdom from his dry and ashen lips, his slow and even gait and the practised movements of his hands made the public consider him a great lawyer.

On the day that he first took his seat on the bench, a junior barrister called Keller was in court. Keller, who could never resist the temptation to make a sarcastic joke, had been called at the same time as Mayne, but had not advanced as far or as quickly as he thought he should or even as he deserved.

Seeing his new Lordship enthroned in dignity, with his scarlet robes about him, Keller reflected for some time, then said to himself loud enough for his companions to hear, 'Well, Mayne, there you are!—there you have been raised by your gravity, while my levity still sinks me here.'

Unfortunately for poor Mayne, who was considered deep, while he was only dark and muddy, his air of 'vapid melancholy' made him Laurel to Norbury's Hardy, Quixote to Norbury's Sancho Panza, and not only encouraged Norbury to greater excesses but unwittingly had the same hilarious effect on the audience as Norbury's deliberate play-acting.

One day a man entered his court and forgot to remove his hat. Mayne rose and pompously pronounced, 'I see you standing there like a wild beast, with your hat on.'

The laughter lasted for fifteen minutes.

In the old days of the County Courts in Ireland, recorders and County Court judges wore bob-wigs and silk gowns, but no robes were worn by counsel. There was not even a convention to enforce the donning of a black coat, but the senior members of the court shuddered when loud check suits or blazers were paraded, though no refusal of audience was possible.

Nonetheless, it was not prudent to disturb a judge's sense of propriety, and serious problems could arise in the hunting season. This was even more so in Dublin. On Saturday mornings the Lord Chancellor used to sit in court to hear applications in lunacy and various minor matters. The Ward Union Hunt met in the neighbourhood of the city on the same day. An ardent sportsman dressed for the meet was briefed to appear before Lord Chancellor Ball. He had changed his red coat for a black one, which was too small to button, and, in wig and gown, rose to address Ball.

'Mr Webb, I cannot hear you,' said the Lord Chancellor. The advocate raised his voice.

'I cannot hear you, sir,' said Ball sternly.

The truth dawned upon the offender and he glanced down at his own display of an upper garment flaming in dazzling hues supplemented by white cord breeches.

'Your Lordship is not suggesting that it is my waistcoat that your Lordship can't hear? It looks loud enough.'

———————

Sir Frank Brady was an ancient Crown Prosecutor who did not believe in overexerting himself. He relied on the Crown Solicitor to call the witnesses and when they appeared he softly whistled a few bars of melody and then read out the deposition that the witness had made before the magistrates. It could never be charged against him that he put leading questions—he put no questions at all. He just read steadily and paid no heed to the consequences. This usually worked to everybody's satisfaction but not always.

On one occasion, he read out,

'Your name is James Flanagan?'

'It is not, sir.'

'And you are a painter?'

'I drive a car, sir.'

The amusement of the spectators and a caustic remark by the Crown Solicitor caused some confusion, so Sir Frank started again.

'Your name is James Flanagan.'

'I told you, sir, it is not.'

'And you live at 14 Pope's Quay?'

'I don't know the place at all, sir.'

'And you are a painter.'

'I am not a painter, sir. There's not a painter in my family.'

'What are you saying?'

The judge had had enough.

'He appears to be contradicting you, Sir Francis.'

Sir Frank peered short-sightedly at the deposition in his hand and then looked at the witness.

'Then I must ask your Lordship's leave to cross-examine him out of his deposition.'

'It does not appear to be his deposition. This witness when sworn said that his name was Pat Reilly.'

Sir Frank did a double-take and shuffled through his papers.

'Oh, I beg your Lordship's pardon,' he exclaimed, more from courtesy than because he was upset by his discovery, 'I appear to have turned over two pages by mistake. This isn't James Flanagan at all.'

Judges were not always so lenient. Lord Peter O'Brien had in mind a protégé who was waiting for Sir Frank's job. This in itself was a tedious occupation. At the age of eighty, the distinguished baronet, instead of resigning, married a new wife and got a new lease of life for another twelve years. Naturally, O'Brien was irked.

An old recidivist was acquitted because Sir Frank got distracted when trying to whistle the top note in the prelude to the third act from Masseult's *Thaïs*. He turned over too many pages and called only the tail end of his team of witnesses. He had often done this before but on other occasions had been put back on the rails. Peter O'Brien, however, saw his chance.

'Have you closed your case?'

'Oh, I think so, unless your Lordship desires to hear some more evidence.'

'I am not here to advise the prosecution. Have you closed your case?'

'Yes.'

He sat back and set to work to recapture that elusive top note.

'Gentlemen of the Jury,' O'Brien thundered, 'you have to find the prisoner not guilty and I have to discharge him. It is a grave public scandal. There can be no doubt of the man's guilt, but by the gross incompetence of the conduct of the prosecution case, the material witnesses have not been called.'

Afterwards, back in the robing room, a colleague sympathised with the old fellow, but his sympathy was not needed.

'I don't give a darn, young man; it does not worry me. I get my fee whether he is convicted or acquitted. Besides, a fellow like that will start stealing again as soon as he leaves here and I'll get another fee to prosecute him at the next assizes.'

Judges are still human and a little kindness from the bench can go a very long way:

A solicitor travelled over to the county town one Tuesday morning in the expectation that he would finish his business in half an hour. Unfortunately for him, an accused, who had been expected to plead guilty, had changed his mind and a case which had been supposed to last twenty minutes threatened to drag on for several days.

The solicitor met friends, as one does when the judge is

in town, and one drink borrowed another until there was nothing for it but to book into a hotel for the night. This, of course, led to the need for a cure in the morning and another hard day's drinking while waiting for the criminal case to finish. By Thursday, he had drunk up and was fed up. He was befuddled and annoyed and losing money. He stumbled into the court and, to their dismay, pushed his way in among the barristers. Suddenly, when one of the latter had just sat down, he jumped up and, swaying like a tree in a hurricane, bellowed at the Bench. 'I've got an application!'

The judge stared at the solicitor but he was not to be stopped.

'I've got an affidavit too. And it's a good one. It's all here. Will you let me open it, in the name of God?'

The judge remained silent and the solicitor fumbled with the papers in his hand. It took time to get them right side up and then, when he tried to read them, it was obvious that the words were swirling around before his eyes.

'In the manner, nah, the Salad Lands, the Settle beds, nah, in the . . . bloody hell . . . .' He flung the papers at the bench and shouted, 'Here, read the effing thing yourself!'

Everyone waited for the heavens to fall but the judge quietly asked that the affidavit be passed to him and read it in silence.

'Order granted,' he said, 'and three days' costs.'

In reverential wonder, his friends escorted the solicitor from the courtroom.

———

Patrick Lindsay had a case in Green Street Court House and his client was on legal aid. For various reasons, he felt that a short sharp closing speech would do the trick and it did. His client was acquitted.

When he came in to the robing room afterwards, he found the prosecuting counsel and his own solicitor red-faced with laughter.

'What's the joke?' asked Lindsay. 'You're certainly taking

your defeat in a good spirit.'

'It's not that,' said the prosecutor. 'It was two fellows in front of me coming out of the court. You know, two of the regulars. They were discussing our performances and one of them sniffed and said to the other, "There's legal aid for you. I often heard Lindsay talking for a good hour—only eleven and a half bloody minutes today."'

Judges can be puzzled like anyone else:

Just after the Second World War, Patrick Lindsay was appearing in a rape case and the defence was consent. At that time, because of the fighting in Burma and restrictions on imports of all kinds, everything made of rubber was of very poor quality. He established that the elastic in the girl's knickers was not pre-war and so, by implication, not very strong. He asked the complainant why, if she had been fighting so strenuously to protect her virtue, the elastic in her bloomers had not snapped. Her naive but honest answer was, 'I lifted it myself'.

This established consent and Lindsay's client was acquitted.

After the trial the judge sent for Lindsay and asked, 'Lindsay, how do you come to know so much about the elastic in ladies' undergarments?'

'I have four sisters, Judge.'

'Sorry for asking,' said the judge.

And judges can be understanding:

Once before Lord Kilwarden (who was subsequently mistaken for Lord Norbury and murdered in Thomas Street by Robert Emmet's followers), John Philpot Curran and Jonah Barrington were moving to set aside the verdict on grounds which they considered to form a most important point upon legal principles.

Curran had concluded his speech, and Barrington was stating what he considered to be the law of the case, when Lord Kilwarden, impatient and fidgety, interrupted him.

'God forbid that should be the law, Mr Barrington.'

'God forbid, my Lord,' answered Barrington, 'that it should *not* be the law.'

'You are rough, sir,' exclaimed Kilwarden.

'More than one of us has the same infirmity, my Lord.'

'I was right, sir,' said Kilwarden.

'So was I, my Lord,' returned Barrington.

The judge fidgeted again, and looked haughty and sour. Barrington thought he would break out, but he only said, 'Go on, sir! go on, sir!'

Barrington proceeded, and whilst he was speaking, Kilwarden wrote a note, which was handed to Barrington by the tipstaff. It said:

'Barrington,

You are the most impudent fellow I have ever met. Come and dine with me this day at six. You will meet some strangers, so I hope you will behave yourself, though I have no reason to expect it!'

They killed the wrong judge.

A young barrister was appearing before the Court of Appeal. He had been speaking for about an hour round and round the question and it was obvious from the pile of papers before him that he was good for another few hours.

The Chief Justice interrupted him and asked him to state the 'gist' of his argument. The barrister looked at his notes. He looked at the bench. He shook his head in wonder that they had obviously failed to grasp anything.

'It is all gist, my Lords,' he explained.

On one occasion, a witness was either shy or surly and did not answer questions in the clear and ringing tones that elderly judges like to hear. The reluctant witness was asked what he had seen at the time of an alleged accident.

'I saw fuck all,' he growled.

The judge put down his pen and looked at counsel.

'*What* did your witness say just now, Mr McGilligan?'

'He said "fuck all", my Lord.'

'Oh? I could have sworn I saw his lips move.'

William Boyd took no hostages when he was fighting a case in court. A unionist himself, he had defended nationalists whenever he was briefed to do so. This did not always please Catholic judges, who had switched political allegiance to obtain preferment. Boyd did not hide his equally low regard for them.

Lord Peter O'Brien was a typical example of a nationalist who had jumped ship and one morning, when Boyd was defending a member of the Irish Parliamentary Party, he was being particularly obstructive. It did not do him any good because Boyd gave as good as he got until O'Brien protested.

'Docthor Boyd, Docthor Boyd, remember your duty to respect the court!'

Boyd matched anger with anger.

'I'll pay to the court the exact amount of respect it deserves.'

BAR v. BAR

Just as bar and bench are doomed to clash, so in the intense competitiveness of life in the courts, it is inevitable that lawyers are tempted to score off each other and, when they do, it usually makes for a good story.

A rough diamond barrister named Egan was never remarkable for the correctness of his English. In speaking to some motion that was pending, he used the word 'obdurate' frequently. Jonah Barrington happened to laugh.

Egan turned round and then, addressing himself to Chief Baron Yelverton, said ironically, 'I suppose, my Lord, the gentleman laughs at my happening to pronounce the word "obdurate" wrongly?'

'No, my Lord,' said Barrington. 'I laughed only because he happened to pronounce it right!'

When Tim Healy's opponent, James Campbell, the future Lord Glenavy, actually managed to weep real tears, while making his final speech to the jury, Healy began his own address with the words, 'Gentlemen of the jury, you have just seen the greatest miracle since Moses struck the rock and brought forth water.'

John Devlin was notorious for inveigling young barristers into going into court for him in dodgy and embarrassing cases. If by a miracle they were successful, he would take the credit. If the skies fell on the victims, he could say to the solicitor, 'What can you expect of these young fellas. Now, if I only hadabeen free . . !'

On one occasion, he approached an older man, Barry Lehane who had been a legal officer in the army before coming into the Law Library and had no experience of practice whatsoever and little general law. He had no work at all in the Library. Devlin explained that to Lehane that he was up to his eyes in two other cases that morning and needed someone to fill in for him for half an hour in the Supreme Court. He, Devlin, promised to be over to relieve Lehane as soon as he was freed from the Circuit Court.

'I wouldn't have to address them?' asked Lehane nervously.

'Are you mad? You'll have the great Cecil Lavery himself to lead you. I tell you you'll be just like a spear carrier in *Aida* in the Gaiety. You won't have to open your mouth. Bring in a few papers and look busy. It'll make a great impression.'

Lehane was nervous but tickled at the same time by the thought of being seen in the Supreme Court with one of the leaders of the Bar. He proceeded duly to the Supreme Court but, to his horror, when the call came, 'Silence, all stand', there was no Lavery to protect him.

His horror intensified when the Registrar called his case. Nobody spoke, nothing happened. The Chief Justice, a stern man, looked down and saw Lehane and asked him if he were the appellant.

Lehane had a tendency to stutter. The agony of appearing before the Chief Justice triggered his disability as quickly as a pollen-laden breeze blowing over a sufferer from hay-fever.

'M . . . m . . . m . . . mLo . . . mLo . . .'

The Chief Justice sighed as only judges can sigh.

'M r . . .?

'Le . . . Le . . . Lehane, mL . . . mL . . .'

'Are you the appellant?'

'N . . . n . . . not in the w . . . w . . . way you th . . . th . . . think.'

'I was not aware that you were privy to my thoughts. Either you hold the brief or you do not. Is there another case listed of which I have not been informed?'

'N . . . n . . . no, m . . . mLo . . . Lord. M . . . M . . . Mr L . . . Lavery. He's the ah . . . ah . . .'

'I do not see Mr Lavery. I see you, Mr Lehane. You have papers in your hand. You are on your feet. I would appreciate it if you would no longer waste the time of this court. We are waiting.'

Poor Lehane was living the worst nightmare of all barristers, that makes them wake up at night in a cold sweat, to be totally unprepared and on one's feet before a panel of judges.

Lehane started to read the first piece of paper that came to hand. It was the Notice of Appeal and he started to stutter through it in a strangulated voice. It took almost ten minutes to get through the first ten lines. It seemed to Lehane like ten hours. The Chief Justice was not amused.

'Mr Lehane, may I remind you that this is not the District Court in Ballyporeen. Have you the faintest idea what you are about?'

'N . . . no, m . . . m . . . m'Lo . . . Lord. I tr . . . tr . . . tried to t . . . t . . . tell your Lo . . . Lo . . . Lordship, n . . . n . . . not the f . . . f . . . faintest idea. I'm only a sp . . . sp . . . spear ca . . . ca . . . carrier for Mr Lavery.'

Everyone in court with the exception of the Chief Justice and the spear carrier himself was biting his or her hand to stifle laughter when Lehane was apparently saved by the entrance of Cecil Lavery but the Chief Justice was unrelenting. Lehane's submissions were being heard; he had to open the appeal.

Poor Lehane floundered on until finally Lavery had to interrupt on humanitarian grounds. He mollified the C.J., apologised for his absence and opened his case.

Lehane fled from the court, a shadow of the man who

had gone into court forty-five minutes before. He wanted to throw up.

At the back of the court, Devlin, who had been there throughout the proceedings, was waiting for him. Devlin caught him by the arm and hissed indignantly, 'Well, holy God, you made a proper balls of that one.'

Chief Baron Palles, in his youth, was junior to Francis MacDonagh in a chancery suit. MacDonagh added a plea which was successfully demurred to by the other side. Palles had opposed the insertion of the plea.

After judgement had been given against them, MacDonagh turned to his junior, saying, 'Young man, I hope this will teach you to be more careful in the future.'

Francis MacDonagh was also very vain. One day he met in the street a junior counsel who had been with him in a successful case the day before. He stopped the junior and said, 'My dear fellow, I must congratulate you upon the way you steered that case to victory yesterday!'

'Oh, MacDonagh, you are too kind. It was your skill and yours alone that secured our success.'

'No, no, there is no need to be so modest. The victory was yours and yours alone.'

'But I examined only one witness.'

'You did a great deal more. Don't belittle your genius. By one Napoleonic move you secured your victory. I have just visited the Attorney in his office, and he showed me the letter in which you made the recommendation that I should be retained to lead you!'

Palles went on his last circuit in 1915 when he was eighty-four years old. One of the last cases that he tried was *Gethings* v. *Cloney*, a battle between two strong farmers in County Wexford. The case arose over the breakdown of an agreement concerning fencing of a stream which flowed from Cloney's land to Gethings's and was being polluted by Cloney's cattle.

When the action first came on for hearing, counsel concocted another agreement, and the going judge of assize was asked to strike the case out on the grounds that the parties were about to settle. Cloney had second thoughts, refused to execute the settlement and adopted the novel course of suing his own solicitor for negligence. He failed in this action, so a year or two later the case was set down again, this time before the Chief Baron.

Leading counsel for the plaintiff was D.J. O'Brien KC, an able but rather timid man, who was known on the Leinster Circuit as 'Anxious Dan'. He led Tom Bodkin, who later, as Professor Thomas Bodkin, became famous in the world of art criticism and Director of the National Gallery. The defendant had a very strong legal team.

O'Brien was hesitant about going before Palles with a case in which the merits were disputable and in which he had such formidable opponents. He suggested to his instructing solicitors, who were known locally as 'The Corsican Brothers', that the case might well be settled. Bodkin advised against this because of the previous agreement.

Dan O'Brien had hardly begun to state the plaintiff's case when, from the opposite side, there arose a chorus of interruptions referring to the settlement from which Cloney had backed out.

After a while Palles remarked, 'See, see, Mr O'Brien, I'd like to look at this settlement.'

Anxious Dan replied obsequiously, 'Of course, anything your Lordship wishes to see we will only be too pleased to show.'

Since the draft deed would show the weakness of the case, there was a hurried whisper from Bodkin: 'He has no right to see it. It is not pleaded. It has nothing to do with our case.'

At that, Dan rather lost his head and, turning to the

Chief Baron, exclaimed, 'My Lord, my junior does not think you ought to see it.'

The Chief Baron shook with amusement and replied, 'Mr O'Brien, do nothing which you think your junior would not approve of.'

For the rest of the trial, almost every question asked or statement made by Anxious Dan was followed by *sotto voce* whispers from the opposing side:

'Does your junior know you're out?' 'Have you got your junior's say-so?'

A barrister died and it was learned that his coffin had been buried in a grave which was eighteen feet deep. Some colleagues were wondering why the gravediggers had gone so far.

'Obviously,' said a member of his circuit, 'they had learned what we all knew, that deep down there was some good in him.'

An ancient barrister was very long-winded but was given considerable latitude by the otherwise impatient Chief Baron Palles. An opponent tried to cut him down by suggesting sarcastically that his knowledge of practice was out of date and took little note of such statutes as the Common Law Procedure Act, to say nothing of the Judicature Acts.

The barrister, Hyacinth Plunkett, replied: 'I admit, my Lord, that it is many years since I was called to the bar. One of the advantages of those days, my Lord, was that it was very difficult for anybody except a gentleman to be admitted to our profession.'

In the old Irish County Court, a judge could give a decree or he could dismiss a case without prejudice, which meant that there was some curable defect which the plaintiff could remedy and then sue again. This was known as D.W.P. He could also dismiss the case on its merits and the matter was at an end. This was known as D.O.M.

Patrick Daniel Flemming, a barrister from the Galtee Mountains, was on circuit in Kerry. To fill in the time on a long summer evening, he and another barrister visited the local graveyard and spent an hour reading the inscriptions on the tombstones.

Eventually Flemming complained, 'Yerra, dem tombstones is very long-winded.'

His friend assured him. 'We'll avoid that in your case. We'll just put

> P.D.F.
> D.O.M.
> R.I.P.'

DRINK

To mark the advance of the spirit of democracy as understood by English liberalism, there were added to the roll of Justices of the Peace between 1892 and 1896 a great number of persons whose judicial qualifications consisted in what was called their popular sympathies; in other words, they were nominated by the local MP, instead of by the Lord Lieutenant. The standard of JP in Ireland was never high. The office had for generations been the preserve of the Ascendancy, and 'Justice's justice' was a byword for maladministration.

As a corrective to this, there was let loose on the community a regiment of the lowest order of politicians, and in many cases of the meanest standard of training and education. They became known as 'Morley Magistrates' and in a short time the phrase passed into the category of abusive language.

The problem of the menu of a JP's lunch, or indeed the question of whether or not he should have any lunch at all, would often depend on the result of licensing applications. The real contest would arise in applications with regard to houses in small villages or *clochans*. The police would oppose these. It was impossible for the constabulary to supervise the liquor traffic in remote clusters of cottages at the tops of glens or in the middle of moors. If one licence was granted in such a locality, the holder could be relied upon to practise all the known methods of canvassing magistrates to keep out a rival. In the same way, a man who had corruptly obtained a licence for a 'wayside' house on a lonely road would have to exert himself, lest he be outflanked and have his custom intercepted at either end. And the motor-car had not even been invented.

Lord Morris was a sturdy and successful advocate and, as he said himself, solicitors would give him any fee not to have him against their client because, whatever about winning, he had a way of devastating a case.

When he was an old man, and his son was MP for Galway borough, the county magistrates were sitting at the courthouse on the subject of renewing licences for public houses.

The Lieutenant of the county, under the influence of a gaunt wife who was a rabid teetotaller, came to the meeting with strict orders from her to suppress all the public houses possible. An astute priest, deep in politics and very opposed to the Morris clan, was cute enough to make use of these principles of the Lieutenant's wife for his own purposes. As each case for renewing the licence came up, he had some reason why it was not to be renewed, his private reason being that the applicant was a Morrisite. Anti-Morris applicants appeared to get their licences on a special plea.

Martin Morris was present and was horrified at the result. All his political friends were being knocked out. He scribbled a hurried note to his father, who happened to be in the Galway County Club nearby. Morris senior was, of course, a magistrate but seldom sat on the bench. Down he walked to the courthouse, with the curled lip of a bulldog ready for a fight. He joined the other magistrates on the bench who could hardly have been delighted to have a former Lord Justice of Appeal among them. The anti-Morrisite priest was not pleased, too, and with good cause.

As the next case for renewal came on, Morris spoke out, emphasising his broad Galway accent to demonstrate the no-nonsense quality of his views.

'In a street where there are already six or seven or more public houses, do ye think that by shuttin' up one, and leavin' the other five or six open, ye are makin' a nation sober? No, nor the neighbours sober either. By the shuttin' up of some, you are just puttin' a premium on the others, and creatin' an estate of value for the ones left that they would not otherwise have had. It's musical chairs ye are playin' with other people's property, and I am not here to countenance such injustice.'

The priest slipped away and the Lieutenant of the county, followed by the other magistrates, voted for every licence that came up to be renewed. They even allowed several new licences.

EVIDENCE

The following is a picture of Ireland before television (from The Last Serjeant *by A. M. Sullivan).*

How the people loved the courts. The litigants 'had their names in the papers'. The clever things the witnesses kept up their sleeves for unsuspecting cross-examiners would be talk of the countryside. The witness who was not cross-examined was always offended. His truthfulness might be challenged without disturbing his equanimity, but to treat his testimony with neglect was a wound inflicted on his sense of importance which might be much greater than his sense of truth. The man who evaded a dangerous question had something to boast about in every public house he visited for a month. Even the defeated found sympathetic listeners for the explanation of the disaster.

A description of Ireland. One hundred years ago or yesterday?

Everyone agreed that perjury was a shocking sin. In certain circumstances. For many years, profound theological discussion raged among patriots as to whether any power in heaven or on earth could release an oath of fidelity to a murder society.

A barrister was briefed to defend a man accused of poisoning someone with a cup of tea. After a conviction at the first trial, he successfully got a new trial in the Court of Criminal Appeal because the judge had misdirected himself in law. In two subsequent trials the juries failed to agree and the accused was acquitted.

Some time later, he was asked by a layman. 'Come on now, tell us the truth. What do you really think? Was he guilty or not?'

He replied, 'Not guilty on the verdict of twelve good men and true. If, however, I were offered a cup of tea in that house, I would be very slow to take it.'

A purveyor of false testimony was called an 'Aliboy'.

A witness, being cross-examined as to his means of livelihood, stated that he had little more than his old-age pension.

'You look a very young man to be drawing an old-age pension,' said the judge. 'Are you seventy years old?'

'Sure I'm not, me Lard, but I'm nearly sixty.'

'And how did you get the pension?'

'Well, me Lard, I just got an oul' Aliboy from the mountains to go in and get it for me.'

A shopkeeper in a small village in Cork found that his till was being systematically robbed. He could find no grounds for suspecting anybody. Coins were never taken, but bank notes disappeared and if any scraps of paper, invoices or envelopes were left in the till they disappeared too.

On a number of occasions, the man, his wife and their four-year-old child would go out in a very public manner and leave the house and shop open—but on these occasions nothing happened.

One day, his daughter, Mary Anne, said to him, 'If I give

you a letter, will you give me a sweet like Mrs McCarthy?'

'Mrs McCarthy has you spoiled,' laughed the father and thought no more about it until looking in through the window of Mrs McCarthy's shop he saw Mary Anne going in behind the counter, pulling open the till a few inches, putting in her hand, pulling out a note and bringing it to Mrs McCarthy, who rewarded her with a sweet.

When Mary Anne came home, her parents questioned her and she told them everything quite openly. For every 'letter' taken from her father's till, Mrs McCarthy gave her a sweet. Some days previously a £10 note and two single notes had disappeared. Inquiries revealed that Mrs McCarthy had paid some bills in the meantime but no one would give details for fear of being branded as informers.

In an appeal at the assizes in a County Court action to recover the £12, the child told her story, corroborated by her father. It was not enough. The defendant had paid in bank notes three small bills the day after the money went missing. In each case the recipient of the money swore that the note paid to him was a single note. The action failed.

One of those witnesses, an ostentatiously devout man, identified with all movements of charity and patriotism, was later heard to boast that it was certainly true that the note handed over to him was a 'single' note but that its value was £10.

Holy Ireland, how are you!

———————

The County Court judge of West Cork once brought along a young English friend nominally as his Registrar, but with the understanding that the duties of his office would be discharged by the Deputy Clerk of the Peace. By some chance, however, the stranger was the only officer present when a burly farmer got up on the table and picked up the bible.

'Swear him,' said the judge.

'Who me?' exclaimed his young friend.

'Yes, you. Hurry up!'

'Oh, I say,' exclaimed Clarence, screwing in his monocle

and looking up helplessly at the mass of humanity towering over him.

'You know you've got to tell the truth, you know the truth the—aw—truth, the County Court truth so help you God.'

The witness kissed the book with enthusiasm. This sounded like the sort of truth he had always intended to tell.

From The Last Serjeant *by A. M. Sullivan*:

Disregard for the truth in the witness-box and in the jury-box was widespread and shocking, but what was worse was the fact that nobody regarded it as wrong. When Dr Kelly became Bishop of Ross he was staggered at a state of affairs which was not peculiar to any diocese but was characteristic of all. The more scrupulous witnesses avoided kissing the bible, and kissed their thumbs before giving false testimony; and indeed persons with very tender consciences used ambiguous words or certain set phrases in place of direct lying in plain terms. A pregnant woman always told the truth, so cases dependent on her corroboration were postponed until she was fit for falsehood. Female witnesses were accused of fraudulent inclusion of a pillow in their attire in order to simulate the condition of truthfulness.

Dr Kelly commenced a crusade. He implored his flock to abandon litigation and to submit their quarrels to arbitration in order to avoid the public scandal of notorious perjury. His neighbour, the Bishop of Cork, instituted an inquiry among his clergy and was assured that the sin of perjury was unknown in the confessional. As for Dr Kelly's crusade, it created prejudice against him among his own flock. They had never heard such a row over such a trifle; this craving for truth appeared to them to be unorthodox. They wondered if Dr Kelly was a Protestant.

A Mr Justice Jebb sentenced two prisoners to death but omitted to direct that their bodies should be buried in the precincts of the jail. A day or two later, in open court, but in the absence of the prisoners, he added the words which he had omitted.

Six out of the ten judges of Ireland to whom the case was referred held that the sentence was thereby rendered illegal, and the prisoners were pardoned and discharged.

In that case lives were saved by what might seem to the layman a technicality. A slander case once failed by reason of a classic demurrer, or objection, on the score of legal insufficiency.

The words 'Sir Myles Cusack struck his cook on the head with a cleaver, and cleaved his head. The one part lay on the one shoulder, and another part on another,' were held not to be slanderous.

It was held that as 'notwithstanding such wounding, the party may yet be living,' and since there was no direct allegation that the cook was killed, the action must fail.

The Irish, American, Canadian, Australian and Indian legal systems are all based on English common law. Now, although the law of all these countries originated in English law, over the years (leaving statute law aside) each of these countries has developed its own body of legal precedent based on the decisions of its own courts. This body of knowledge has been built up through the system of legal reporting and the printed volumes of law reports.

Unfortunately, for many years there were no printed reports of Irish decisions available in Ireland, so Irish lawyers had to rely on the books of reports that came over by mail-boat from England.

There is a story of a barrister who was pleading in the High Court in Dublin on a tricky point of law.

The judge was almost convinced but needed, and wanted, to be pushed a little more before he would commit himself.

'Are you sure, Mr Plunkett,' he asked, 'that what you have stated is the law?'

The advocate pulled his watch out of his waistcoat pocket and examined it.

'Unquestionably, it was the law half an hour ago, my Lord. But, by this time, the package boat has probably arrived from England and I shall not be positive until I see what it has brought with it.'

———————

Of course, not everybody is convinced of the absolute merits of this doctrine of precedent. When followed blindly, it can lead practitioners up very blind alleys, particularly when the judges and lawyers of one country look over their shoulders at what has become another jurisdiction.

A few years ago the late Mr Justice Niall McCarthy gave a splendid warning against such behaviour:

Forensic forelock-touching is as much a part of the cultural cringe that has beset our country as the mimicry of English accents and manners, but it may be more damaging in its long term effects . . . It is really since I have sat on the bench that I have become so aware of the degree to which the citation of precedent is made a substitute for reasoned argument and analysis of principle . . . It is the reason for the decision that is important, rather than the decision itself. If the reasoning be defective, then the leather binding of the Law Reports does not give it authenticity or merit.

———————

Jonah Barrington, writing more than one hundred and sixty years earlier, is of the same opinion and has a swipe at judges at the same time:

The doctrine of precedent was based on the notion 'that an ignorant barrister (whose opinion nobody probably would ask, or, if obtained, would act upon) immediately changed his character, should he by interest, subserviency, or other fortuitous circumstances, be placed on the judicial bench—all the books in his library pouring their information into his head!

The Great Seal and the King's patent were held to saturate his brain in half an hour with all that wisdom and learning which he had in vain been trying to get even a peep at during the former portion of his life, and the mere dicta of the metamorphosed barrister were set down by reporters as the infallible, but theretofore inexplicable, law of the land, and as such handed round to other judges under the appellation of precedents, entitled to all possible weight in judicial decisions.

This old doctrine of the infallibility of dicta and precedents, which presented, in fact, an accumulation of enigmas and contradictions, was at one time carried to great lengths, I believe partly from a plausible system of making legal decisions uniform, whether right or wrong, and perhaps partly from the inability of the adapters to make any better sort of precedent themselves.'

County Cork was always a great county for legal disputes and Kanturk was one of its most litigious towns.

The Kanturk man was supposed to think of all problems from the point of view of possible litigation. The traditional happy Kanturk man was pictured as one who in life swore his way to triumph over his enemies and after death was translated to a court in which his testimony obtained perpetual credit. The bad Kanturk man, of course, went through life swearing clumsily and contradicting himself and losing his cases, and eventually he was condemned to be eternally decreed with costs on the higher scale.

The one thing that a Kanturk litigant prided himself on was his corroborative evidence. His artistic appreciation realised that, to be effective, his own evidence should appear to be modest and diffident and the convincing stuff should come from an outside source which would, of course, be completely disinterested. Material corroboration was considered to be best of all.

Unfortunately, so much effort was sometimes concentrated on corroboration, that a plaintiff forgot about proving the most basic elements of his case. One Kanturk plaintiff, in an action for assault, triumphantly produced a piece of cloth from his pocket. He claimed that the defendant had knocked a bit out of his skull and, unwrapping the cloth, revealed the bit.

He lost his claim, however, because, in his anxiety to introduce the fragment of bone, he had forgotten to point out the man who was alleged to have chipped it off. The defendant came into the box, swore that he was not even at the fair on the day and, in the absence of identification, the case failed.

A claim to a substantial property was once put forward, based on a deed alleged to have been executed in Kanturk. The people resisting the claim suggested that the document had been forged three years after the death of the grantor, but the evidence in favour of the proper execution appeared to be unimpeachable.

A most respectable old farmer had witnessed the signing, to which he duly testified.

'You seem to have wasted a lot of wax making this big seal,' remarked the judge.

'Well, my Lord,' said the witness, ''tis not all wax; we put in a new farthing to make a big seal of it.'

'There's no sign of anything in the seal.'

'Oh, 'tis there, 'tis there. I remember well, my Lord, we put in a new farthing.'

'Well, I'll test your evidence by that,' said the judge, and he took his penknife and started scraping away at the wax.

'The witness is quite right,' he said, 'there is a farthing in this wax.'

He scraped a little more.

'. . . dated three years later than the deed.'

A junior barrister once applied in the old Exchequer Division for liberty to amend a writ. As issued, it was endorsed with a claim for the trover and conversion of some household goods and a goat. Leave was sought to add a claim for a quantity of manure.

Judge Murphy ruled that the addition was unnecessary since the word 'goat' implied a quantity of manure.

There was once a very pernickety judge, let's call him Judge O'Needler, who would go to extreme lengths to pick holes in a case when in a bad mood. One day a Motion for Further Consideration was before him concerning the distribution of the assets of a deceased person.

O'Needler interrupted counsel in the middle of his application. 'Hold on, Mr Kehoe, you haven't proved the man was dead.'

'There's no question of it, m'Lord. He's dead all right.'

'So you say but where is the death certificate?'

'There is none, my Lord. They're a bit lackadaisical round here in that regard as you know yourself.'

'Mr Kehoe, what I know personally is not evidence.'

'This case has been going on for years and no one has ever even suggested that the poor man wasn't dead.'

'That may be so, Mr Kehoe, but who is to say that they are not all mistaken. This man could be in Manchester. He could be in Boston. May I remind you and everyone here for the hundredth time that this court does not operate on hearsay or conjecture. If you want to present a case in my court, you will do so on the basis of proven facts. That's enough now. Case dismissed, costs against your client.'

Kehoe had had enough also. 'If you want proof I'll give it to you.' He turned and called out, 'Come up, Arthur Cox.'

Cox came into the box and took the oath.

'What is your name?'

'Art Cox.'

'Did you ever have a brother called Mikey.'

'I did surely. He was the oldest in the family.'

'Where was Mikey Easter two years?'

'Wasn't he in bed in the room with the stomach?'

'Did the doctor see him?'

'Ah God, he did. Dr Quinn. There was nothing he could do for him. "Send for Father Spring, Art," he said. Of course, he was a great age. I'm not young meself. '

'And what did Father Spring do?'

'Gave him Extreme Unction what else. The wife had everything prepared in the room. Then we said the Rosary. But he was gone before we finished.'

'Who had gone? The priest?' asked the judge. 'Be more precise.'

'You're saying Mikey died?'

'Don't lead,' snapped the judge. 'Don't answer that question, Cox.'

'Did anything happen to Mikey? Just tell the judge exactly what happened.'

'What happened? Mikey died on us there in the bed.'

'How does this man know he was dead? Will Dr Quinn give evidence?'

'I know a dead man when I see one. He was as stiff as a plank by the time the wake was over. The whole townland saw him.'

'And then what?'

'We put him in the coffin.'

'Did you do it or did you only hear that it had been down.'

'I helped lift him in myself.'

'And that put the lid on it as you might say?'

O'Needler looked up rapidly but Kehoe was poker-faced.

'What then?'

'We removed the remains to Killnalack chapel.'

'And what happened next day?'

'Wasn't there Mass for the poor craythur?'

'And Father Quinn prayed for Art Cox?'

'Who else would he pray for?'

'And then?'

'We buried Art.'

'Was there any other funeral that day? You didn't by any chance follow the wrong coffin?'

'Mr Kehoe!'

'There was no other funeral that day.'

'You saw the coffin buried?'

'I did surely and so did half the parish.'

'Was a decade of the rosary said?'

'It was said by our cousin, Father O'Brien.'

'Did you see the grave filled up? There were none of those fancy green things that they cover graves with?'

'I wouldn't know about them. The grave was filled by Mick Higgins and Packy Ross.'

'Is there a gravestone on the grave?'

'There is.'

'And when it was being erected, there was no sign that the grave had been disturbed?'

'Mr Kehoe!'

Kehoe looked at the witness and then stared at the judge. 'Don't answer that but answer me this. Have you seen your brother since?'

There is an improbable but true story told in legal circles which illustrates the maxim 'If at first you don't succeed, try, try, try again.'

At the turn of the century, a barrister from Belfast was not doing too well before Mr Justice Holmes, who interrupted him with traditional judicial weariness.

'Mr MacFarlane,' he remarked, 'that was your eleventh point and it is as bad as the other ten. Have you any more points?'

The Belfastman was honest but persistent.

'Well, my Lord, I do have one more point to make. I don't think much of it myself but you can never tell what a Court will think of any point.'

He made his submission and won on the last point!

———————

Age has a tendency to exaggerate human characteristics. The carefree become slapdash. The precise become finicky. Judge McQuaid fell into the latter category. No sloppy thinking or careless phrasing were allowed in his court.

A process server stepped into the witness box. Doing his job. All routine.

'Service on wife in dwelling house, your Honour, on first March,' he sang out.

McQuaid looked over his spectacles. 'You swear that the woman you served was the wife of the defendant?'

'I believe so, your Honour.'

'But, God bless my soul, you have just sworn it!'

The process server was taken aback and stumbled over his reply.

'Well, your Honour, 'tis the way that she have the appearance of being his wife.'

'What appearance is that? If she had the same appearance as the defendant, God bless my soul, she might be his twin sister.'

'Sure, he have no twin sister, your Honour.'

'How do you know that? Were you present at his birth?'

'I was not, your Honour. But she do have the name of being his wife.'

'It's not good enough, sir, not good enough. But I'll accept it and the responsibility, may I add, is yours.'

His parting look implied awful consequences.

———————

'You are old, Father William.'

Very often, crown prosecution work was the only source of income of certain ancient barristers, and their colleagues at bar and bench made every effort to ensure that this source did not dry up. In one case, a senior Crown Prosecutor was, in fact, senile for six or seven years before his death and only the fees of his office stood between him and the workhouse. His comrades raised a small fund for his immediate needs and put his prosecutorship out to commission. It was arranged that all his duties would be discharged by some of the younger members of the mess, while the old gentleman agreed that he would robe and sit in court without interfering in the conduct of his cases.

Unfortunately, one day after lunch his current substitute was delayed but somehow the absence was not noticed. The first witness for the defence was put in the box. This was a local doctor who never lost an opportunity of advertising his own high opinion of himself and whose weakness in this respect was a by-word in the town and did not enhance his popularity.

Defence counsel sat down and the old man rose to his feet.

The judge and the members of the circuit were horrified, but there was nothing that they could do beyond sending clerks out to scour the building for the missing junior and praying that nothing too awful would happen.

'Tell me now,' said the old man. 'Are you a doctor?'

The doctor was taken aback but recovered his aplomb quickly enough.

'Certainly I am a doctor.'

'Are you a good doctor?'

The witness allowed himself a self-deprecating smirk.

'Oh, you cannot expect me to give an opinion on that.'

'Are you a good doctor?' the old man repeated.

The judge, playing for time, indicated that the witness must answer the question.

'Well, in that case . . .' the doctor replied and responded

to the chance of a lifetime. 'I am widely known not only in this city or indeed in this country from all parts of which I have been fortunate enough to receive innumerable expressions of admiration for my work. I have published many excellent and interesting articles on professional topics that have circulated throughout the world, and have elicited congratulations from the highest authorities in every quarter of the globe. Therefore, without expressing any opinion of my own, I may say that, in the universal estimation of the members of my profession, I *am* a good doctor.'

The old man looked at him for at least five minutes while everyone held their breath.

'Arrah, go home, you old fool,' said the senior Crown Prosecutor, a phrase which so happily coincided with the sentiment of the court that no notice was taken of it.

In Bandon once there was an action for goods sold and delivered. The plaintiff conducted his own case, which left a lot to be desired and any half decent defence would have allowed the judge to hold for the defendant. Expectantly, therefore, he encouraged the defending solicitor.

'Well, Mr Quill, you have heard—sniff—the facts as set out by the plaintiff. What is your defence?'

'Your Honour,' said Mr Quill, 'these were probably goods supplied to the wife without authority.'

The plaintiff called out, 'I'm not married.'

Pause.

'Well then, your Honour, I rely on the Statute of Limitations.'

The judge consulted his papers.

'The goods were supplied this year, Mr O'Brien.'

Mr Quill was a man of infinite resource.

'I mean, of course, your Honour, the Tippling Act.'

Up popped the plaintiff.

'This was all hardware. I don't sell drink.'

Mr Quill was growing desperate.

'What about the Sale of Goods Act?' he suggested in a tiny voice.

The plaintiff had prior experience of the law.

'Sure, he walked off with the stuff,' he reminded the judge, who by this time was growing impatient.

'Ah, Mr Quill,' he exclaimed, 'instead of making absurd suggestions, put up your client and let him tell us what his defence is.'

Mr Quill was now on surer ground.

'It's like this, your Honour,' he explained. 'I had to suggest every sort of defence because my client has not come in to instruct me properly.'

The judge was disappointed, but he was also annoyed.

'Then, I'll decree him,' he declared bluntly.

'Sure, your Honour, you can't do that. Isn't he dead? He was buried yesterday.'

A young barrister arrived in Limerick on circuit for the first time and was briefed for the defence by a friendly solicitor, who assured his nervous counsel that he would have no trouble whatsoever with the case in which it was alleged that goods had been sold and delivered to their client.

'Open and shut, Mr Lawlor,' said the solicitor. 'A piece of cake.'

'I'm glad to hear it, Mr Kinsella,' said the barrister, glancing at his skimpy brief, 'and what exactly is the defence?'

The solicitor looked at him with the air of a man propounding an unassailable truth.

'The defence, sir, is the plaintiff.'

This was a point of law that had not been covered in the King's Inns.

'I'm not with you, Mr Kinsella. I'm sure you're quite right, of course, but how is the plaintiff a defence?'

With the tolerance of an old hand for a neophyte, the solicitor explained.

'The plaintiff, sir, is a registered blackguard!'

Such rough Limerick justice has been described as 'the outlawry of the unfit'.

Sir Edward Carson, the famous barrister and politician, had a client who had been grievously defamed. The defendants had justified and, in furtherance of their defence, tried to show that he was something of an adventurer living entirely upon his wife's fortune. Carson's case was that there is every difference between a man who exploits his rich wife and the man, who having married a rich woman, allows her to help him.

The plaintiff had been handled very severely in cross-examination. When it was his wife's turn to be cross-examined, the first question was: 'When did your husband last do a day's work?'

She did not know.

'Your husband is wearing a very handsome astrakhan coat. Where did he get it?'

She had given it to him.

'Who paid for the Rolls Royce you arrived in this morning?'

She had.

'How much money did he put up towards the purchase of your mansion in the country?'

Nothing. And so on.

It was time for re-examination. Carson lifted up his long, lean body, smoothed his silk gown, turned his melancholy face towards the lady and said,

'Mrs Jones . . .'

In a sad weary tone, as if the whole matter were very painful to him, he continued, 'Mrs Jones, were you in love with your husband?'

In the circumstances, no answer but one was possible. 'I was,' she replied faintly.

'Is there any one of these things about which my friend has asked you which you regret?'

Once again, only one answer was possible.

'No.'

'Mrs Jones, if the opportunity arose again today, would you be proud and happy to do it all again?'

'I would,' she cried, lifted by her advocate to enthusiasm.

'Thank you, Mrs Jones.'

The jury gave Carson's client £5,000.

A similar example of skilful examination arose in the case of Major Yelverton and Teresa Longworth. She was a beautiful girl of good family who had volunteered to go out as a nursing sister to the Crimea in the 1850s. In the course of her travels she had met the major and love at first sight was followed by a form of marriage. The parties lived as man and wife for some time until the major, who had unexpectedly inherited a fortune, saw the opportunity of making a very splendid match for himself if he could only disembarrass himself of poor Teresa.

The case was litigated under various headings in Ireland, England and Scotland. In Ireland an obliging butcher sued the major for the price of meat supplied to the lady. If he were her legal husband he would be liable to pay for her necessaries. He set up a defence that any relations between himself and the lady amounted to nothing more than a mere flirtation, and the alleged marriage ceremony was only a joke incidental to the pleasant dalliance.

At the conclusion of the defendant's examination in chief, Sir Edward Sullivan asked, 'Major Yelverton, did you ever love Teresa Longworth?'

The major started; he had not expected this and he foresaw a trap. But only one answer was possible, so he straightened himself and said, 'Yes, of course I did.'

Sir Edward looked at him quietly, then after a slight pause more deliberately than ever, he asked 'Did you ever love her honourably?'

And there was the major, impaled upon the horns of a dilemma from which there was no escape. He twisted and turned through several answers, but the upshot of it all was that, unless he were to admit himself to be a designing seducer devoid of all honour, he was bound alternately to admit that he had gone through this ceremony of marriage because without it Teresa Longworth had refused to be his.

An Irish jury found no difficulty in finding for the butcher, which meant the establishment of the honour of the lady.

With their usual perversity, the courts of England and Scotland, subsequently, took a different view.

A brief arrived in the Law Library from a solicitor in County Clare.

The barrister read it and was not impressed until he came to the final sentence: 'I am not very hopeful. I do not believe our client is right about this, but, of course, something may go wrong.'

An old lag was having a consultation with a fresh-faced barrister. The evidence against him was overwhelming and there was no way the barrister could see to get an acquittal.

'Mr Redmond,' he said, 'the only thing I can suggest is that we plead guilty, throw ourselves on the mercy of the court and hope that the judge is in a good mood.'

Redmond smiled the condescending smile of the experienced for the novice.

'Ah, no, sir, I don't think we'll plead guilty, sir. That could be foolish now, sir. You never know, there might be something they can't prove.'

What a lot of trouble would have been saved if Morann's Collar had been available in quantity over the centuries as a means of control over judges and witnesses.

It belonged to Morann, the foster son of the smith Mahon and son of King Cairbre of the Cat's Head, and, if anyone put it around his neck when he was giving judgement, it would squeeze the life out of him if he gave a bad judgement and would only ease up when he gave the correct verdict.

In the same way, anyone who wore it and gave false testimony would also be choked.

———————————

We have said that barristers are players and judges umpires. It has been the general rule that the best players nearly always made the worst umpires. They were too used to having their own way to withdraw from the battle.

One such was Mr Justice Boyd. Once in the 1890s he was hearing a civil bill appeal about a parcel which was alleged to have gone missing while travelling first on the West Clare Railway and subsequently on the Great Southern and Western. The owner had sued the latter company but, because he could not prove that the parcel had ever been handed over to it, his case had been thrown out. During the appeal, a witness told the court that a friend of his had heard a guard tell a porter that he had given a similar parcel to another guard. This was, of course, blatant hearsay, and counsel for the Great Southern protested immediately that it was not evidence.

'I don't want evidence,' thundered the judge. 'I want the truth.'

The judge found for the appellant and gave a decree for £9.

When Boyd was reminded by counsel for the railway that the claim had been for only £5, he said that he would amend his decree.

'You can't,' said counsel. 'There's no machinery.'

'No machinery?' asked the judge. 'Do you see that pen? There's machinery.' And he crossed out what he had written.

Tipperary and Kerry alibis were notorious in the old days. Briefly speaking, in the Kerry alibi the events that were recounted were all true but they happened on the wrong date. In the Tipperary alibi, when the Crown witnesses gave their evidence at the petty sessions, it was all noted down and witnesses were then primed to give evidence that the Crown witnesses had all been somewhere other than where they said they were on the day in question. It was very difficult to break down a Tipperary alibi.

Proceedings, evidence and, accordingly, cross-examination have always been vastly different in Irish and English courts. Apart from the bull-roaring of a Daniel O'Connell, Irish courts have always been much more subtle.

This fact is illustrated by the example of some courts martial in Dublin during the Troubles (the war of Independence in Ireland after World War I) in which an English barrister was prosecuting several prisoners. The Attorney General had been briefed, but was engaged elsewhere. He looked into the court one day and the Englishman asked him to examine one of the witnesses. The witness came to the end of a long and elaborate story which, if true, proved an alibi for the prisoner. The Attorney General put two simple questions:

'Where did you say you lived?'

The witness told him.

'How many doors from the prisoner's house?'

'Next door.'

In Irish terms and before an Irish court, nothing more was needed. Any Irish lawyer would have known that the witness had probably been taken through his story a hundred times, and cross-examined keenly. Every hole in story and alibi would be stopped up; and the more astute the prosecuting counsel was, the more credence he would give to the accused's defence. Irish judges and juries would know this, so all that was needed was to establish any connection between the accused and the witness. This is what the Attorney General had done, but he had forgotten that English officers were not in on the secret and the accused was acquitted.

———————

Eye-witness evidence should be best evidence, but the numerous infamous mistaken identity cases that sully the legal records show that this is not necessarily so.

An outstanding example of the inaccuracy of eye-witnesses is the execution of Mary Queen of Scots. It seems that all witnesses of her death differed in their accounts, except on one detail. They all agreed that the Queen's head had been cut off by a single blow of the executioner's axe. It now appears that when the body was exhumed in the last century, pathologists demonstrated that it had taken three strokes to separate head and body.

This discrepancy was cited by Maurice Healy when defending some highway robbers in Clare or Limerick. The prosecutor said nothing until the end of his own speech, when he finally exploded.

'And as for Mary Queen of Scots, we all know that she was the Queen of Sorrows, but little did she think, when she laid her head upon the block in Fotheringhay Castle, that three hundred and fifty years later she would be summoned from the tomb to provide an alibi for the highway robbers of Coolanellig Wood!'

———————

In these days, when confessions, even signed ones, have been demonstrably as unreliable as they ever were, circumstantial evidence is often called into play. But it, too, needs to be treated with caution and with tempered commonsense. Perhaps, however, the commonsense of Lord Morris was too evident in his remark to two counsel whose arguments about the nature of evidence had been unnecessarily long-winded:

'When I see a man coming out of a public house wiping his mouth on his sleeve, well, that is *prima facie* evidence.'

A judge called William O'Brien had a crier called Ford who, like a court favourite (pun intended), exercised an extraordinary influence on him affecting all his judgements, feeding him information and opinions about the accused, sometimes in their favour and sometimes not.

In one case before O'Brien, a man called Brown was charged with murder arising out of an allegation that he had helped his sister's husband to murder the latter's mother, sister and brother and shove them down several wells. The case against Brown was largely one of suspicion. But in those days, it was not a question of a right to remain silent; prisoners could not give evidence at their own trial. Some story had to be presented for the prisoner and it was customary to back this up by witnesses who would be put through the rigours of cross-examination. The alternative was to rely on the weakness of the Crown's case.

It was never easy to decide which course to take, and the skill of the advocate depended on his ability to make this decision. In this case, Brown had a large number of witnesses to back up his defence and his two counsel had taken the decision to call them. Just as they were about to do so, the judge's familiar hissed to one of them, 'Mr Adams, *call no evidence in this case.*'

Naturally, they understood this to mean that the judge did not think that the Crown case stood up and, after some confusion, they told O'Brien that they intended to call no evidence.

This seemed to satisfy His Lordship.

'O-oh, a most important and momentous decision, Misther Adams,' he informed one of the barristers, 'no doubt you have considered it carefully?'

This worried them a bit, but Ford had spoken, so they resolved to be bold.

'My Lord, I have,' said Adams.

The judge began his charge to the jury.

'Gentlemen of the jury, you have listened with careful attention to the speech of Misther Adams, and you now know full well, even if you had not known before, the exact case which the prisoner desires to be presented on his behalf. Gentlemen, it will, no doubt, have occurred to you, as it has occurred to me, not once but many times, that if there were one word of truth in that story, there must be sitting in this court or within easy summons of it a large number of persons who could have gone in that witness-box to swear to its genuineness; and *not one witness has been called for the defence!*'

Adams yelped. When O'Brien had retired, he went berserk. He had to explain to the judge in chambers. He had to take a train to Dublin to interview the Lord Lieutenant. He had to go to London and ask for an audience with the Queen.

Fortunately for him and for Brown, the verdict of the jury was 'not guilty'. Adams actually fainted and long after everyone else had gone he sat with his head in his hands. When Ford came out of the judge's chambers, Adams leapt at him and started to strangle him.

'For the love of God, Mr Adams, let go of me,' gurgled Ford, 'you're choking me.'

'You ruffian,' roared Adams, 'you infernal blackguard! What do you mean by telling me to call no evidence?'

'Mean?' asked Ford in self-righteous indignation. 'Mean? Sure, Mr Adams, you know well that *I can't abide perjury!*'

———

An Irish witness was giving evidence in Liverpool. The judge was not impressed by him and asked, 'Tell me, Murphy, what happens in Ireland to a witness who does not tell the truth?'

'Gor, me Lard, I think his side usually wins.'

———

In former days the County Galway grand jury met in Galway city before each assize. It was composed of the county gentry and transacted other local affairs to do with the county. At one of these meetings late in the afternoon, after the usual gargantuan grand jury luncheon, a shy backward country boy was being questioned with very little response. He would say 'Yes' and 'No' to practically the same questions.

The foreman of the grand jury grew impatient. He was thinking of the one and only train, due to leave shortly, which would convey himself and most of his brother jurors to their homes at the east side of the county.

'Look here, child,' he interrupted, 'do you know the nature of an oath?'

The child did not reply.

'And do you know that if you tell a lie, you will go to Hell and we will all be late for the Mail?'

An Irishman was a witness at a trial in Westminster Hall in a case about something that had happened at dinner in a house where he dined frequently. In cross-examination, he was asked how he could possibly recollect a particular date when he dined there so often. His reply would have been understood in Ireland, but it foxed them in Westminster.

'Recollect it?' he exclaimed. 'How could I forget it? We had roast shoulder of mutton, in July, without new potatoes!'

A young lady at Cork Assizes was giving evidence for her employer in an action against a grocer whose product had given the employer food poisoning. She said, 'I made known to the shopkeeper the purpose for which the goods were required so as to show that I relied upon his skill and judgement.'

'You what?' asked the judge unbelievingly.

'I made known to the shopkeeper the purpose for which the goods were required so as to show that I relied upon his skill and judgement.'

'My goodness,' said the judge, 'Where were you at school?

'The Convent of Mercy here in town.'

'What remarkable nuns! How long have they had the Sale of Goods Act in their curriculum?'

EXPERTS

The most general ground for attack on a will was an allegation of mental incapacity on the part of the testator. A clever and dramatic witness, without going very far from the actual truth, can contrive to give an account of the daily happenings of normal life in a manner which will convey that he is describing the antics of an idiot.

It was in will suits, almost as much as in accident cases, that the medical expert shone. They never stated anything that was untrue; indeed they rarely stated anything that was not in fact commonplace, but there were artists in the profession who could state the commonplace with its infinity of contingencies and possibilities in terms that would make a jury's flesh creep. The harrowed feelings of the palladium of liberty would urge them to agree upon a verdict quickly lest before their eyes the apparently lusty plaintiff in an accident case should develop all the symptoms described as possible, or lest the horrors of the testator's delinquescent brain by contemplation might affect their own.

Sometime in the last century, Seymour Bushe, Alex Sullivan and an unnamed solicitor were wrangling over the chances of defeating a will on the grounds of insanity. Tim Healy, their leader, slept by the fire during their debate. Finally, he woke up, announced that he was going home and said, 'I'll show you how to win this case. Have you twenty-five guineas?'

'I have my cheque book, Mr Healy.'

'That will do. Come along.'

Sullivan and Healy walked home in their usual style, manoeuvring around one another like battleships because each was deaf in the same ear. The poor solicitor followed, wondering what was going to happen to him and his cheque book. They had not gone far when Tim halted and turned to the solicitor.

'Do you see that hall door? Take my brief and your cheque book, go inside and give the brief and a cheque for twenty-five guineas to the gentleman you will meet in there. Tell him he is to come to the Court of Exchequer at two o'clock tomorrow and he is to prove that the testator was mad.'

The case came on before the Chief Baron and a jury. Although the Chief Baron had great affection for the expert, he was determined to cross-examine him. But cross-examination only made the testator appear to be more insane than ever and repeated cross-examination aroused in the mind of the jury some suspicion of the Chief Baron's own sanity.

The expert was that prince of Dublin surgeons and most companionable of men, Johny McArdle.

'Mr McArdle,' cried the Chief Baron, 'you never saw this man, yet you tell us that you have formed the opinion that he was insane.'

'Certainly, I never saw the man—I mentioned at the outset that I had never heard of him three days ago, and my evidence is mainly based upon these two postcards that I hold in my hand. I have been told that they were written by the testator. Perhaps they were not. If they were not written by the testator, my evidence is of little value. Assuming that they were written by the testator, they show manifest signs of insanity. Note the calligraphy. Does your Lordship notice that the tails of the letters droop downwards, and the 'y' at the end of 'whiskey' has drivelled away into nothing —that is most characteristic. It implies an organic defect in the motor sensory area just here'—and Johny turned the back of his head and put his finger on his scalp.

'There is evidence,' protested the Lord Chief Baron, 'that he was tipsy when he wrote that postcard.'

'That would make him worse,' said Johny solemnly,

'when that particular spot of the brain becomes affected. Drink hastens its decay. Note also, my Lord, he slips out words. Look at the last line—"Don't forget to bring a whiskey". The quantity of whiskey is left out. It might be a gallon or a naggin. It is dreadful to note a symptom like that. It is agraphia. He never meant to write "a".'

'He may have meant to insert the word "bottle",' suggested the judge.

'I would not like to take the responsibility of saying that —it is too serious. It would show that cerebral degeneration had reached its most dangerous phase. He must have been subconscious of the fact that if he tried to write "bottle", he would probably have written "hippopotamus" in spite of himself. This is confirmed by the evidence of *aphasia* that I have heard was very marked.'

'What evidence was that?'

'His friend Patrick Healy came in to see him and he addressed him as Robert.'

'In the dusk it is said that he mistook him for Robert Swanton, who had just left him.'

'That, my Lord, confirms what I say. He would probably have called you Robert or me Robert. Having once said Robert, he would have to keep it up. This indicates that a large patch of the dexter motor sensory area is permanently damaged.'

The dexter motor sensory areas of the jury suffered sufficient temporary damage from this evidence to ensure a disagreement.

American visitors are sometimes taken aback when they hear Irish people talking about Galway hookers. Terms of art in one area often have an unfortunate meaning to outsiders. Another example is the word 'stripper', which definitely does not have the same meaning in Rathkeale as in Soho.

In the old days, cows were sold 'engaged free and fair to be clean calved by the 5th April'. Sometimes the cow refused to milk free and fair. Sometimes, the 5th April was long gone before the calf made its appearance. But the worst of calamities occurred when a cow never calved at all and settled down to eat its purchaser out of house and home. This was a 'stripper'.

An almost equal calamity can occur when an urban judge is required to adjudicate over matters agricultural.

There was a delightful old gentleman in Limerick, by profession a solicitor, but by occupation a farmer, whose expert knowledge caused him to be engaged in most cases where cattle had failed to live up to their pre-sale hype. Whenever he cross-examined a resourceful defendant, the old gentleman's bald head would shine, his face flush, his waistcoat expand as he warmed to the fray. As with most people who know a particular subject intimately, it was inconceivable to him that there could exist people in the universe who were not as aware as he was of the intricacies of the cattle trade.

Surfeit of knowledge frequently leads to incapacity of expression and old Ryan was no exception.

'I am quite satisfied that there was a breach of contract,' said an inexperienced judge, 'but, Mr Ryan, you have given me no proof of damages.'

'Proof of damages, your Honour? Why she was a stripper—a stripper, your Honour.'

'Yes, but what do you suggest is the loss your client has suffered?'

'Loss, your Honour? The loss is terrible. Consider, your Honour, what this means to this poor man. She was a stripper.'

'But what is the measure of damages?'

Ryan could not conceive that there could be anyone on earth so stupid as not to understand the enormity of what he was saying.

'Your Honour! Your Honour! My God! Wasn't she a

stripper, and your Honour wants proof of damage!'

'Twenty shillings,' said his Honour.

The dumbfounded Mr Ryan could only gasp.

A psychiatrist was giving evidence on behalf of a plaintiff who was suffering from a traumatic neurosis as a result of an accident.

'This must have been a difficult case. How did you manage to help this man?' asked counsel for the defendant.

'I put him at his ease. I did my best to put him at his ease, stop him worrying.'

'And how did you stop him worrying?'

'I told him that things would work out, that he'd be well in no time.'

'And how would things work out?'

'You know, he'd win his case, get a settlement and he'd be well then.'

'That's very interesting. So this is how you cure people? You tell them to look for compensation and once the money's in the bank, hey presto, they're up and about.'

'You're putting it badly but in a crude way the principle is correct. My patient was suffering from anxiety. A court case aggravates this general paranoia. Remove the particular anxiety and the general neurosis disappears.'

'But what about chaps who aren't pursuing a claim in Tort?'

'I'm not with you.'

'Mentally ill patients who are not simultaneously litigating in the hope of a handsome award from a sympathetic jury.'

The psychiatrist shook his head, 'No. I've never had a patient like that.'

Mr Arthur Chance was a distinguished orthopaedic surgeon and a professional witness. It was almost impossible to upset his conclusions.

He was once called to give evidence in an action to terminate an award of Workmen's Compensation in Tipperary by reviewing the original order on the grounds that the workman had either wholly or partially recovered and was fit to work again.

When the assembled solicitors and regular court *aficionados* saw Mr Chance entering the witness box, the odds against the workman rose sharply. Chance began his evidence with practised ease.

'I have examined the applicant in this case, Gobnet O'Kennedy. He claimed to have injured his back while lifting a heavy object. He now complains of excruciating pain whenever he attempts to work. I carried out the normal examinations in these cases and asked him to perform certain standard physical movements and exercises such as leaning forward, touching his toes and so on but he claimed to be quite unable to perform any of these acts, yelping as if in agony whenever I insisted that he make an effort. In short, if his account were to be believed, this man would be almost totally immobile.'

'And do you agree with that, Mr Chance?'

'I do not.'

'And why not?'

'Because O'Kennedy undressed before the examination and dressed himself again afterwards and on neither occasion did I observe any inability to move freely or to make full use of his muscles. It is my professional opinion that Gobnet O'Kennedy is fully fit for work.'

It might have been Moses bringing the tablets of stone down from Mount Sinai. Chance in upper case had made O'Kennedy's chances very lower case indeed.

Nevertheless, Gobnet's counsel had to go through the motions.

'I'm calling Mr O'Kennedy's GP, my Lord.'

The local doctor was self-evidently not a fashionable Dublin surgeon. He looked as if he would have been more at home with his arm up a cow's behind or driving a tractor-load of muck than wielding a stethoscope. There was more than a whiff that he might have supped late the night before.

'Dr Kerrigan, in your expert opinion is Mr O'Kennedy fit for work?'

'Not on your life. That poor man will never work again. The back is done for entirely. Heavy work now would finish him.'

'Can you tell me precisely what is the matter?'

'Took on something beyond his capacity, you see. Gor yes, muscles and vertebrae, sore and strained. He's a great lad and I've known him all his life. Never afraid of work. He'd tackle anything and that was the ruination of him. It's a terrible case. He should have known better but the likes of Gobnet O'Kennedy, they give it all they've got. All his people are the same. Decent good people. He's done for himself now and that's a fact.'

The insurance company's counsel may have been an irresistible force but Dr Kerrigan was an immovable object. The fiercest question failed to shake his conviction that Gobnet was practically a basket case. Counsel was compelled to call on higher authority.

'Did you hear *Mr* Chance?' with heavy emphasis on the surgical 'Mr'.

'Oh, I heard him all right.'

'Everybody in the court-room . . . it would be fair to say everyone in Ireland knows Mr Chance's reputation as the country's foremost orthopaedic surgeon. With all due respect, Dr Kerrigan do you consider yourself qualified to contradict him?'

'That's very fine and well, I'm not disputing Dr Chance's knowledge of bones but, God bless you, bones have nothing to do with it. It's the muscles, don't you know, the muscles he's ripped.'

'He can't work?'

'Not labouring work and that's all he's educated for.'

Counsel went in for the kill.

'You heard Mr Chance say that O'Kennedy removed his

trousers with no difficulty whatsoever. What do you say to that?'

'That it's a funny class of work you'd be looking for with your arse bare to the world.'

———

Richard Lalor Sheil, playwright, politician and journalist, in his entertaining book Legal and Political Sketches (1855) *does not stoop to impartiality. If he does not like somebody, he lets it be known. He did not like Mr Leslie Foster of County Louth, barrister, scholar and Commissioner for Education, anti-Catholic and anti-Union:*

Foster was another man, like Judge Mayne, who cultivated gravity. It was said that he acquired the habit during a stay in Constantinople where he met the Grand Signior and ever afterwards retained an expression of dignity which he copied from the Reis Effendi, if not from the Sultan himself. He also held himself out to be a person of very various and minute erudition. In every drawing room, and at every dinner table at which he appeared, no matter what topic was introduced, he took the opportunity to air his knowledge. If he found a boy whipping a top, he would stop to explain the principles upon which it was put into motion. He was versed in all the points of science connected with the playing of marbles. Should he come across a pair of bellows, he would begin a dissertation upon the structure of the human lungs.

This pedantry did not always meet a sympathetic response. In due course Foster became a judge and one day, in a revenue case, a medical witness was giving the result of his study of a certain deposit of chemical substances.

'In fact, Dr Apjohn,' interrupted Baron Foster, 'the substance was only mud.'

'Perhaps,' replied the doctor drily, 'your Lordship would favour the jury with the definition of mud?'

———

The stones of the road can tell us about Sherlock Holmes's dog that did not bark, but I wonder do these non-readers know of his brother Baron Dodd's dog.

A Serjeant Armstrong was cross-examining a hand-writing expert in Green Street court-house and growing increasingly exasperated.

Suddenly he snapped a question at the expert.

'But what about the dog, Mr Madigan?'

'What dog?' asked the expert. 'I don't know anything about a dog?'

'The dog that Baron Dodd said he wouldn't hang on your evidence?'

GREAT SPAKES AND CURIOSITIES

Language and its use, written and spoken, construed, analysed and abused, is the essence of the law and the art of the lawyer and many are the great 'spakes' that have come down to us over the years, whether in judgements or off-the-cuff retorts.

The following tribute by Maurice Healy, barrister, royalist and bon viveur, to two old Irish judges, is a gem:

Each of them was bathed in the waters of the common law, and looked upon statutory enactments as a bather might consider the limitations of his pool, or the dam that contained his waters.

John Mitchel, a solicitor, was not a political friend of Daniel O'Connell's, but recognised the old man's qualities, as can be seen in this passage from the introduction to his Jail Journal *(1854).*

Two distinct movements were stirring the people: one open and noisy—the Catholic Relief agitation; the other secret and silent—the Ribbon and Whiteboy movement. The first proposed to itself the admission of professional and genteel Catholics to Parliament and to the honours of the professions, all under London law; the other, originating in an utter horror and defiance of London law, contemplated nothing less than social, ultimately political revolution.

For fear of the last, Great Britain with a very ill grace yielded to the first. Unfortunately for Ireland, Catholic emancipation was carried in 1829. 'Respectable Catholics' were contented and became West Britons from that day.

At the head of the open and legal agitation, was a man of giant proportions in body and in mind; with no profound learning, indeed, even in his own profession of the law, but with a vast and varied knowledge of human nature, in all its strength, and especially in all its weakness; with a voice like thunder and earthquake, yet musical and soft at will, as the song of the birds; with a genius and a fancy, tempestuous, playful, cloudy, fiery, mournful, merry, lofty and mean by turns, as the mood was on him, a humour broad, bacchant, riant, genial and jovial; with profound and spontaneous natural feeling, and super-human passions, yet withal, a boundless fund of masterly affectation and consummate histrionism; hating and loving heartily, outrageous in his merriment, and passionate in his lamentations, he had the power to make other men hate or love, laugh or weep, at his good pleasure—insomuch that Daniel O'Connell, by virtue of being more intensely Irish, carrying to a more extravagant pitch all Irish strength and passion and weakness, than other Irishmen, led and swayed his people by a kind of divine, or else diabolic, right.

Mitchel was well able to criticise O'Connell.

He led them, as I believe, all wrong for forty years. He was a lawyer, and never could come to the point of denying and defying all British law. He was a Catholic, sincere and devout, and would not see that the Church had ever been the enemy of Irish freedom.

He was an aristocrat, by position and by taste, and the name of a republic was odious to him.

He passes a final judgement.

O'Connell died heart-broken in 1847; heart-broken not by a mean vexation at seeing the power departing from him; the man was too great for that; but by the sight of his people sinking every day into death under their inevitable, inexorable doom. His physicians ordered him to a warmer climate, in vain: amidst the reverent acclamations of Paris, through the the sunny valleys of France, as he journeyed southward, the B'anshee wail followed him and found him, and rung in his dying ear. At Genoa he died: ordering that his heart should be taken out of his dead body, and sent, not to Ireland, but to Rome; a disposition which proves how miserably broken and debilitated was that once potent nature.

If John Mitchel had stayed in Ireland and attained some office in an Irish republic, it would have been for the best if it had not been Minister for Justice. Here are his views on the reformation of offenders:

What to do then, with all our robbers, burglars and forgers? Why hang them, *hang* them. You have no right to make the honest people support the rogues, and support them better than they can support themselves. You have no right to put a premium on villainy and put burglars and rick-burners on a permanent endowment.

In criminal jurisprudence, as well as in many another thing, the nineteenth century is sadly retrogressive. 'Reformation of offenders' is not the reasonable object of criminal punishment, nor any part of the reasonable object. Jails ought to be places of discomfort; the 'sanitary condition' of miscreants ought not to be better cared for than the honest, industrious people—and for 'ventilation', I would ventilate the rascals in front of the county jails at the end of a rope.

———————

In Jonah Barrington's time, the late eighteenth and early nineteenth centuries, there were two famous judicial brothers, William and Robert Johnson. William we have already met as the unwilling judicial brother of Lord Norbury. Robert has been written about by many authors because he was one of the few judges who came close to impeachment. This was because William Cobbett published some anonymous pamphlets of his and then, to avoid prosecution himself, revealed his sources. Johnson was the subject of a highly dubious refugee felon motion and was legally 'kidnapped' to stand trial in England.

The following anecdote is about their father:

Old Mr Johnson, the father of these two gentlemen, when upwards of sixty procured a diploma as a physician, to make the family genteeler. He was a decent ordinary good kind of apothecary, and a very respectable, though somewhat unostentatious doctor; and, above all, a good orthodox, hard-praying Protestant. I was much amused one day after dinner at Mr Hobson's, at Bushy Park, near Dublin, where the doctor, Curran, myself and many others were in company. The doctor delighted in telling of the success of his sons Bob, Bill, Gam and Tom the attorney, as he termed them; he was fond of attributing Bob's advancement rather to the goodness of Providence than that of the Marquess of Downshire; and observed, most parentally, that he had brought up his boys, from their very childhood, with 'the fear of God always before their eyes'.

'Ah, 'twas a fortunate circumstance indeed, doctor,' said Curran, 'very fortunate indeed, that you frightened them so early.'

Barrington's description of Judge William Johnson:

He was the only one of my brother barristers whose smiles were not agreeable to me when we went on circuit together. I liked his frowns extremely, because they were generally very sincere, extremely picturesque, and never niggardly bestowed. But as my own smiles had the trouble of mounting up from my heart, whilst he had an assortment ready prepared to take a short cut to his muscles whenever policy required, I found that in this particular we were not equally matched.

A certain barrister was called 'The Scrooger' behind his back because of his ability to avoid standing his round in public houses. Ernest Wood, a sharp-tongued leader of the bar after World War II, was in the downstairs bar of the Four Courts one day and was offered a glass of champagne by The Scrooger. He accepted and, to his even greater surprise, was offered another and yet another. Recognising a miracle when he saw one, he drank all three.

When at last he made his excuses, he asked someone why your man was being so liberal.

'He's just been appointed to the High Court. Hadn't you heard?'

'No, he hasn't,' Wood contradicted his informant. 'Kennedy has. The Scrooger doesn't know it, but he's celebrating the feast of the passover.'

A father and son went down to their local and had seven pints of stout each. On their way home, they were short-taken and relieved themselves in a narrow passage-way beside a neighbour's house. The neighbour brought an action for nuisance.

The judge found for the plaintiff and declared, 'It is a principle of the common law, of Roman law and the law of nations—a principle recognised in the pandects, in the Code Napoléon, in the American Constitution, and in the teachings of Confucius, that a man should sneeze where he buys his snuff!'

Once upon a time, a person about to be committed to a mental hospital had to have two peace commissioners, a doctor and some policemen in attendance when the deed was being done. Among the many forms to be filled in was one in which the peace commissioners certified a fee of one guinea for the doctor.

In exceptional cases a fee of two guineas might be recommended and in the case of a man called McGinty in Galway, one of the peace commissioners, a friend of the doctor's, approved this increase. The other peace commissioner, for sheer spite, changed the figure back to one guinea.

The form was then given to the doctor but, as soon as he saw the alteration, he threw the paper to the ground and leapt at the begrudger. Within seconds, there was a general melée, bodies rolling around on the floor, fists and boots flying, the thud of knuckles on bone in counterpoint to lurid Galway obscenities.

Over the din could be heard the voice of poor McGinty. 'For God's sake, min, would ye not have sense. I'm supposed to be the madman.'

Justice Kelly loved the world and the world loved him. Nobody ever enjoyed his existence with more cheerfulness and composure.

'Egad!' he used to say, 'this world is wheeling round quite too fast to please me. For my part, I'd rather be a young shoe-boy than an old judge.'

This analysis of the problems of the Irish bar in 1827 was relevant for many years (from Richard Lalor Sheil's Legal and Political Sketches*):*

The principal cause of the calamities of which so many examples occur at the Irish bar lies in the unnatural elevation to which the members of that body are exalted by the provincial inferiority to which Ireland is reduced. The absence from the metropolis of the chief proprietors, and indeed of almost all the leading gentry, has occasioned the substitution of a kind of spurious aristocracy. An Irish barrister is indebted for his importance to the insignificance of his country; but this artificial station becomes eventually a misfortune to those who are dependent upon their daily exertions for their support; and who, instead of practising those habits of provident frugality, which are imposed by their comparative obscurity upon the cloistered tenants of the two Temples in London, become slaves to their transitory consequence; and, after having wasted the hard earnings of their youth and manhood in preposterous efforts of display, leave their families no better inheritance than the ephemeral sympathy of that public, whose worthless respect they had purchased at so large a cost.

The life of an eminent Irish lawyer may be rapidly sketched. He is called without any other property than those talents which had not in general a descendible quality. For some years, he remains unemployed; at last he gets a brief, creeps into the partialities of a solicitor, and sets up a bag and a wife together.

Irish morality does not permit the introduction into the chambers of a barrister of those moveable objects of unwedded endearment, which Lord Thurlow used to recommend to the juvenile members of the profession; and marriage, that perpetual blister, is prescribed as the only effectual sanative for the turbulent passions of the Irish bar.

In the spirit of imprudence, which is often taken for romance, our young counsellor enters with some dowerless beauty into an indissoluble copartnership of the heart. A pretty pauper is almost sure to be prodigal. If Mrs O'Brallaghan, the wife of a mere attorney, provokingly displays her amorphous ankle ascending the crimson steps of her carriage, she must do so too even though she may have 'ridden double' at her Aunt Deborah's. A carriage cannot be brought into an obscure street, an alley or a cul-de-sac. There is such a bargain to be had of a house in Merrion Square. The lady discovers a taste for furniture. The counsellor is raised to the dignity of King's Counsel and his lady is initiated into the splendours of the Viceregal court. She issues cards to half the town which is an intimation that she is 'at home'.

In the meantime, she has been prolific to the full extent of Hibernian fecundity. The counsellor's sons swagger it with the choicest spirits of Kildare Street. The young ladies are accomplished in musical and literary affectation. The passenger is arrested in his nocturnal progress by the crowd of brilliant vehicles before the door, the blaze of light, the din of extravagance from within.

But where is the counsellor all this time? He sits in a sequestered chamber and pursues his midnight labours by the light of a solitary taper, scarcely hearing the din of pleasure that rolls above his head.

The wasteful splendour of the drawing room, and the patient drudgery of the library go on for years. The counsellor is at the top of the forensic, and his lady stands upon the summit of the fashionable, world.

At length death knocks at the door. When the hour of agony is at hand, the loud and heartless voice of official insolence echoes from chamber to chamber. The sheriff's officers have got in; his majesty's writ of *fieri facias* (to seize the goods of the dying man) is in the process of execution; the sanctuaries of death are violated, the blanket and the silk gown are seized together. After having charmed his country by his eloquence, and enlightened it by his erudition, he breathes his last sigh amidst the tears of his children, the reproaches of his creditors and a bailiff's jest.

An Irish barrister transferred to England after independence and built up a large practice. He was asked how this had happened. He was a foreigner, he did not know the English mentality, how could he have succeeded in their courts?

'The legal world in England,' he replied, 'is an alien world within society. It requires no knowledge of the psychology of the people, but proceeds on its way by rote. The bench is exclusively composed of men who have grown up in the artificial atmosphere of the ruling class, the public school, the university, the well-provided apprenticeship to the Inns of Court, lucrative practice and the accumulation of wealth. None have ever suffered that excellent corrective of theoretical opinions, hunger for want of the price of a meal. That all knowledge of English psychology was unnecessary was certainly an advantage to me, a stranger coming among them.'

Although Serjeant Sullivan was quite successful at the English bar, he claimed that he had two overwhelming disqualifications for practice there.

First, he insisted on dealing with his cases in his own way. The successful English barrister conducted cases in the way he was told. The solicitor or the managing clerk in charge of the case delivered a number of minute instructions as to the points to be made and method of presenting the case, and in court he sat in front of his leading counsel and gave him commands from time to time in any emergency that arose. The whole purpose of this practice was to increase costs.

Cross-examination consisted in reading counsel's brief to an opposing witness in the apparent hope that he would agree, although in his direct examination he had contradicted it. It took time, and the most important thing from the point of view of the instructor was that plenty of time should be taken. It added to the costs.

A country curate was appointed bishop. This leap-frog form of promotion did not commend itself to Paddy Flemming, a barrister from Tipperary, who had high notions of the rights of seniority.

'Dat's a queer sort of a bishop,' said he, 'squz out of a curate.'

In pre-combustion-engine days, a young barrister asked his master if he should study animal cases and whether or not such study would pay off.

'Well, Billy,' said the master, 'the staple subject of litigation in the High Court is the horse. The best brains of the worst people are incessantly engaged in selling bad horses at good prices, and good prices round here being over £50, that's beyond the reach of the County Court. You can get a good negligence case out of a horse too. Find one that comes round a corner at a furious gallop of ten miles an hour, and you're made.

'The County Court progresses on cows. Sheep never give rise to litigation except when they are worried by dogs. They're so cheap that a man with the finest genius for fraudulent representation would be losing his time dealing in sheep—he would have to tell so many lies for so little money. Pigs, now, are valuable, but, except for the purpose of being damaged by railway companies, drowned by steamship companies, and run over by side cars, they're of no interest to lawyers.'

'And donkeys?'

'Oh they're *ferae naturae*' (wild animals under nobody's control).

Two barrister members of the Irish Parliamentary Party availed of their trips to London to play on the Stock Exchange and made large fortunes. One of them abandoned the bar, took a house in Park Lane, installed a pretty actress, loaded her with diamonds, and drove her about in a beautiful carriage and pair. Meanwhile, he went on speculating.

One evening at Tim Healy's house, John Barry, MP for Wexford, was chatting about old comrades in the party.

'By the way,' he said, 'I've not heard of old Pat for a long time. How is he?'

'Broke,' said Tim Healy. 'Park Lane surrendered, the horses and carriages sold, the lady has transferred her affections to a duke, and Pat has gone back to his wife.'

'Well, well,' said Barry. 'Misfortune does indeed make strange bedfellows.'

It must always be remembered that, in an earlier age, courts were not only palaces of justice or injustice, they were also places of entertainment and, as sure as theatres have their regular first-nighters, the courts had their regular attenders, with more than their fair share of eccentrics and down-right lunatics among them.

Two such characters were regulars in Limerick County Court.

The first was an inoffensive old man, Mr Joyce, whose only eccentricity was that he was convinced that the top of his skull had fallen off and that it was necessary to wear a covering on his head to prevent his brain from catching cold. The other man, Pierce Evans, was given to violent outbreaks.

Whenever they arrived in court, the proceedings would be interrupted while an application was made for leave to Mr Joyce to wear his hat. Over the years, the announcement of the opening of the court was amended to include the final words, 'And Mr Joyce may wear his hat.' This saved a lot of time.

One day, however, in spite of his inclusion in the court ritual, Mr Joyce stood up and sought to address his Honour.

'Yes, Mr Joyce,' said Judge Adams, 'I have already given you leave. Put on your hat and sit down.'

'But I can't, your Honour.'

'Why the devil not?'

'Please, your Honour, last night Mr Evans asked me to dinner, and after dinner he said he had a new game to show me and I let him tie me on the billiard table, but then, your Honour, he beat me with a cue and I shall never be able to sit down again.'

Adams glared at the two of them for a minute.

'I wish to God the bugger had killed you. Then you'd be dead and he'd be hanged and I'd be rid of both of you.'

The manager of the claims department of an insurance company was in Galway one day. Paddy Lindsay had heard that he was engaged to be married and went to congratulate him and to learn something about his intended. 'This is the best news I've heard in a long day, Bobby.'

'It surprised me, I can tell you.'

'Better late than never. I've no doubt she's a great girl. Where would she be from?'

'Tipperary.'

'You couldn't do better. A great county, the Golden Vale.'

'Better land than Connemara, that's for sure.'

'And her people have land?'

'They have.'

'And a good sized holding, I suppose?'

'About two hundred and fifty acres.'

'Boys oh boys, you're on the pig's back, Bobby. It was worth waiting for. And you'll tell me next she's an only child, you divil you.'

'Ah no, she has brothers and sisters.'

'I see. How many of them?'

'Eight.'

'She'd never be the eldest now?'

'No, she's the youngest.'

Lindsay heaved a deep sigh. 'God and his holy mother take care of you both. You'll be lucky to get the fresh eggs at Christmas.'

A man was charged with operating a brothel in Gardiner Street, Dublin. He claimed that he had nothing but respectable married couples in his hotel and brought the register into court. It showed Mr and Mrs Toomey of Toomevara, Mr and Mrs Gort from Galway, etc. but the State Solicitor called a farmer from Mayo who had been up for a football match in Dublin. His story was that, while having his tea in a cafe in O'Connell Street, he fell into conversation with a young lady. She invited him to go with her to a hotel nearby for a lie-down. He had a couple of hours to kill before his train left so he though he'd go with her just for the crack. She booked a bedroom and they took their clothes off and got into bed.

'And then what did you do?'

'I suppose you could say we started trickin',' said the witness.

'Trickin'?'

'That would be it, all right.'

'Did you finish this trickin'?'

'Well now, we did.'

'And then?'

'I hopped out of th'oul bed and skedaddled.'

'And why did you do that?'

'It struck me that she mightn't be the right sort and that maybe I had no business to be there.'

Even his enemies conceded the physical courage of William Toler 'or rather his recklessness of the lives of others as well as his own' and, even when he was raised to the eminence of Chief Justice of the Common Pleas as Lord Norbury, he betrayed his original tendency to settle matters after the old Irish fashion, at the distance of twelve paces. More than once he told counsel, who was pressing him too closely with a Bill of Exceptions, that he would not seek shelter behind the bench.

On one occasion, a gentleman named Brougham charged him with falling asleep during a murder trial. Norbury's immediate reaction was to threaten resignation and demand satisfaction because 'that Scottish *broom* wanted nothing so much as Irish stick'.

———

L ord Justice Holmes had just sat through a long and intricate action involving a family dispute. The opening words of his summing-up should be carved in stone:

'The Duffy family was very sickly; it was also rather fraudulent. The illnesses from which its members suffered in turn gave the convalescents opportunities to try to overreach the invalids.'

———

I n a landmark negligence case, a four- or five-year-old child was injured while playing on the premises of the Midland Great Western Railway Company.

The author of one of the standard legal textbooks at the time was rash enough to describe the infant plaintiff alliteratively as 'one of a rabble of ragamuffin Irish raiders'.

This elicited an immediate protest from another legal author, who insisted that it be put on the record that the child was, on the contrary, 'the quite presentable son of a respectable chemist'.

———

B arristers have to be ready for every eventuality and have an instinctive knowledge of human nature and people from all walks of life. Daniel O'Connell had this gift. It was said of him: 'Throw him upon any particular class of men, and you would imagine that he must have lived among them all his life, so intuitively does he accommodate his style of arguments to their particular modes of thinking and reasoning.'

Trial by Battle, although, in practice, obselete by the close of the reign of Edward I, was still available down to the time of Henry VIII to anyone accused of felony by a private individual, and was not actually done away with until 1820.

In that year, the Act, 59 Geo. III. c. 46, abolished Appeals of Felony and Trials by Battle. The cause was an Appeal of Felony brought against an Abraham Thornton who had been acquitted by a jury of the murder of a girl called May Ashford.

When called on to plead, Thornton threw his glove on the floor of the court and said, 'Not guilty, and I am ready to defend the same with my body.'

Counsel for his accuser, Mary's brother, cried out, 'Don't touch that glove.' But the court allowed the challenge and, since Ashford refused to accept it, Thornton was discharged.

If Ashford had taken up the challenge, he would have had to fight Thornton with leather shields and cudgels for a whole day or until one of the combatants cried 'craven'.

Dublin in the rare old medieval times saw some spectacular Trials by Battel (sic) (Sir Jonah Barrington).

Single combat was formerly a very prevalent and favourite mode of *administering justice* in Ireland, and not being considered so brutal as bull-fights, or other beastly amusements of that nature, it was authorised by law, and frequently performed before the high authorities and their ladies—bishops, judges and other persons of high office generally honouring the spectacle with their presence.

The last exhibition of that nature which I have read of was between two Irish gentlemen, Connor MacCormac O'Connor and Teige MacKilpatrick O'Connor. They fought with broadswords and skeens (large knives) in the castle of Dublin, in the presence of the archbishop and all the chief authorities and ladies of rank. They had hewed each other for a full hour, when Mr MacKilpatrick O'Connor, happening to miss his footing, Mr MacCormac O'Connor began to cut his head off very expertly with his knife, which, after a good deal of cutting, struggling, and hacking, he was at length so fortunate as to effect; and having got the head clear off the shoulders, he handed it to the lords justices, who were present, and by whom the head and neck was most graciously received.

Whatever about the risk to life and limb, single combat provided a quicker and cheaper solution than a Chancery suit.

In *Knight* v. *The Marquis of Waterford* (1844) it took a litigant fourteen years to carry an appeal to the House of Lords, only to discover that since he had originally started his case in the Court of Chancery, when he ought properly to have started it in a common law court, he must go back and start all over again in the correct court.

This pales into insignificance beside the suit over the castle and lordship of Berkeley in the north of England which lasted from 1416 to 1609.

Judges have been traditionally appointed in Ireland on a political basis. But what would you do if you were a Liberal Prime Minister in 1905 after twenty years of Tory government?

There was no shortage of aspirant judges, but the brightest and the best had become Tories long before. The pick of Liberal judicial material was dead. Others held shaky seats, some were too ancient and were given peerages, most of the remainder were cripples. Many dubious appointments were made, solely on the grounds that the appointees had remained faithful for two decades.

There was also the greatest difficulty in finding politically sound law officers. Redmond Barry was appointed Solicitor General because it was assumed that he was a relative of John Redmond's, and because he had had a hat broken as a young student when heckling a unionist meeting.

In the ottocento, *before the judiciary became 'independent' of the Crown in 1784, judges were sent over from England, partly to protect the property of absentees and partly for political reasons. They were not of high quality, mainly because the salary was minimal. For this same reason, any Irish barristers who accepted appointments to the bench at that time came from the least successful practitioners.*

Baron Monckton of the Exchequer, a typical import from England, was said to understand *black letter* and *red wine* better than any who had preceded him in that situation.

His drunken appearances on the bench seriously outnumbered his sober ones and one barrister said of him: 'Monckton is a most mathematical judge. He always describes the segment of a circle in making his way to the seat of justice!'

For those who succeed, the rewards of the bar have always been great. The bar's public relations machine is never slow to remind critics that the unsuccessful are vastly greater in number than the stars. Jonah Barrington has this to say about those who gave up the law for easier professions:

I remember once remarking to Curran how many men, though all willing, and some competent to work, were destitute of briefs at the Irish bar, yet contrived to make conspicuous, though not over-talented figures in political and diplomatic situations.

'Why, some,' answered he, 'thrive by the gift of common sense; some others by the influence of their wives, and such-like causes.'

Lord Clancarty and Mr Vesey Fitzgerald were two Irish barristers in whom I never could perceive the raw material for ambassadors, yet none ever dropped their *Nisi Prius* (a writ to have a case heard outside Dublin) with better effect. The former, though a friendly, honourable man, seemed particularly ill-calculated to shine amongst the immortal carvers, who at Vienna cut up nations like dumplings, and served round people and kingdoms to the members of their company with as little ceremony as if they had been dealing only with paste and raspberries.

Judgements are like diamond mines. In the thick blue clay, wonderful jewels can be found embedded.

Here is a judicial warning against Elinor Glyn's Three Weeks:

A glittering record of adulterous sensuality masquerading as superior virtue, as it does in this book, [is] calculated, with consequences as inevitable as they are sure to be disastrous, to mislead into the belief that she may without danger choose the easy life of sin, many a poor romantic girl striving amidst manifold hardships and discouragements to keep her honour untarnished.

Justice John M. Woolsey was much kinder about James Joyce's Ulysses.

In respect of the recurrent emergence of the theme of sex in the minds of his characters, it must always be remembered that his locale was Celtic and his season spring.

Woolsey's view was not shared by Judge Manton of the Circuit Court of Appeal, who held that:

Masterpieces have never been produced by men given to obscenity or lustful thoughts—men who have no Master.

A local government auditor had disallowed certain payments by Dublin Corporation in 1894, one item being the cost of a luncheon by members of the Corporation on the occasion of the 'annual inspection' of the Vartry Waterworks. The validity of this allowance came before the Queen's Bench Division on an application for mandamus, *to order the Corporation to pay. The leading judgement was delivered by Sir Peter O'Brien (Pether the Packer):*

Now I think it is relevant to refer to the character of this luncheon. I have before me the items in the bill. Amongst the list of wines are two dozen champagne, Ayala, 1885—a very good brand—at 84s. a dozen; one dozen Marcobrunn hock—a very nice hock; one dozen Château Margaux—an excellent claret; one dozen fine old Dublin whiskey—the best whiskey that can be got; one case of Ayala; six bottles of Amontillado sherry—a stimulating sherry; and the ninth item is some more fine Dublin whiskey!

Then Mr Lovell supplies the 'dinner' (this was a dinner, not a mere luncheon!) including all attendance at 10s. per head. There is an allowance for brakes; one box of cigars, 100; coachmen's dinner; beer, stout, minerals in syphons, and ice for wine. There is dessert, and there are sandwiches, and an allowance for four glasses broken—a very small number broken under the circumstances.

In sober earnestness, what was this luncheon or outing? It seems to me to have been a picnic on an expensive scale . . . a sumptuous repast for the members of the Corporation on the Wicklow hills . . .

The Solicitor General appealed pathetically to common sense; he asked, really with tears in his voice, whether the members of the Corporation should starve; he drew a most gruesome picture; the members of the Corporation would traverse the Wicklow hills in a spectral condition unless they were sustained by lunch. I do not know whether he went so far as Ayala, Marcobrunn, Château Margaux, old Dublin whiskey and cigars. We do not say that the members of Dublin Corporation are not to lunch. But we do say that they are not to do so at the expense of the citizens of Dublin.

A Consultation.

Arrogance and idleness well described one William O'Brien, who practised in Cork in the last century. Clever, yes. Lazy, indubitably. He once had a five o'clock appointment in a solicitor's office in a probate action. Junior counsel and client were there before five. O'Brien turned up at a quarter to six. 'Good morrow,' he began without any preamble, 'that man Michael Connor will be a most important witness tomorrow.'

'You can't call him, Mr O'Brien,' said the solicitor.

'Can't call him? Why not?'

'He's the testator, Mr O'Brien. He's dead.'

'Oh, you know very well I don't mean Michael Connor. I meant James Foley.'

'James Foley is my clerk that served the sub-poenas, Mr O'Brien.'

Silence. The solicitor then stated the obvious.

'You haven't read your brief, Mr O'Brien.'

'Read my brief? Read my brief? And why should I read my brief? A pack of lies! A pack of lies!'

He won his case.

A blessing to litigants!

During a trial in Cork, the prosecutor was Edward Carson. While he was cross-examining, the Right Honourable John Morley, one of the accused, interrupted him, addressed the judge and apologetically explained that through the lantern in the roof he could perceive that the building was on fire over his Lordship's head, and he excused himself for mentioning it on the ground that he thought his Lordship would be interested to know it. The judge thanked the defendant for the interruption and observed that he had been puzzled to know what it was that had been dropping on his notebook, and he now perceived it was molten lead from the lantern.

'It is very nearly one o'clock,' he said, 'and we may as well adjourn a little earlier than usual and call in the fire brigade. I fancy a couple of hours ought to put the matter right, and we will reassemble at half past two o'clock.'

As he bowed to the bar, there was a spurt of flame over his head and Carson made a remarkably quick get-away and was first out of the court. By half past two, flames were pouring from every opening and no vestige of roof or floor remained. It burned like tinder.

That fire was a blessing to many a litigant for many years afterwards. Throughout the county of Cork, at every sitting of the recorder or the County Court judge, whenever a document might not favour a litigant, there was someone to swear that it had been burnt in the Cork court-house. This beneficial state of affairs lasted until someone failed to produce to the Lord Chief Baron a document in relation to which there was proof that it had been executed eleven days after the useful fire.

Oops, Sorry!

Alex Sullivan never forgot a face but had an atrocious memory for names. One morning he rushed into the coffee-room in the Four Courts to gulp down some food between cases, and became conscious of the fact that an extremely familiar face was beaming at him across the narrow table.

As soon as the man addressed him, his musical chant proclaimed that he was a Cork man. Sullivan, sure that he would be interested, said, 'I hear there's great excitement in the South Mall since Gleeson diddled the whole street and bolted.'

'I beg your pardon,' said the man angrily, 'but I did nothing of the kind.'

———————

The Archimedes Principle.

Serious and substantial cases are usually of a simple character. It is the trivial and ridiculous case that induces perspiration, and there is generally some utterly baffling point of law, whose determination invokes prolonged and industrious research.

Patrick Murphy entered the premises of Mr Scully and imbibed a creamy pint. He lingered over his beverage as long as possible since he did not have the means of purchasing a second pint. The condition of his apparel did not enhance the tone of Mr Scully's bar, so Patrick was eventually induced to make room for a more profitable customer.

The only thing that one creamy pint could do for Patrick Murphy was to put a terrible mouth on him for a second or even a third. So, instead of going home like a sensible man, he hung around outside in the hope that someone he knew might come along and do the needful. He loitered on the kerb, wiping his mouth and enjoying the sunshine. Presently, it occurred to him that while he faced the sun, it was the shady part of him that was getting warm, very warm. Before he had intuited what was happening, the seat of his trousers was on fire. He blamed Mr Scully and sued him.

Archimedes is reported to have spent much time and trouble in devising a means of firing the hostile ships that beset Syracuse. Mr Scully had never heard of Syracuse, though on cross-examination he admitted that he had a brother in Syracuse, New York, who was a conductor on the Delaware and Hudson Railway. Nonetheless, in unconscious imitation of the famous Greek, he had, to attract custom, put in the window of his public house an enormous concave mirror, in which persons might contemplate their exaggerated images.

By some mischance, Mr Murphy had put the seat of his trousers into the focus of the mirror which in turn kindled a fire of legal controversy which has never been resolved. There was a consensus that there was negligence on the part of the mirror, but whether or not Mr Murphy's trousers were guilty of contributory negligence was argued for a whole day. At the conclusion the recorder reserved judgement but died before he had made up his mind. The question is still open.

An honourable criminal:

Frank Leeson was the only son of a country gentleman in Ireland who was not good at managing his affairs and was about to be thrown into prison for debt. Frank, who was devoted to his father, was in love with a beautiful young girl of no fortune. He immediately stopped seeing her and married a woman with £8,000 of her own. He paid off his father's debts and entered into the world in some style.

Mr Leeson Senior's health began to fail and he decided that he needed to move to Dublin. He sold his estate and got the money in bills. All Frank's money was in bills too, tied up in bundles ready for the journey to Dublin. Unfortunately, the night before they were due to travel, the house burned down and everything in it was reduced to ashes. They were ruined but travelled to Dublin anyway, Frank hoping to get a position in the army or in some office in the grant of the Lord Lieutenant.

This did not happen. He spent a lot of time in waiting rooms but nothing was offered to him. Soon it came to the point where they had no money for food. Frank was desperate. He left the house and went into the city, where he accosted a wealthy-looking man and demanded money from him with 'such a wildness of accent' that the terrified stranger handed over a purse with fifty guineas in it.

Next day, the robbery was 'noised abroad' and in a short time the police arrested a respectable merchant who had some slight resemblance to Frank. The merchant was sent for trial. Frank Leeson heard of this and wrote a letter to the accused, telling him what he had done and assuring him that if he was not honourably acquitted, he would surrender himself to the law. The poor merchant showed the letter to anyone who would read it, but everyone dismissed it as a trick.

The case duly came up for trial and the merchant was convicted. The judge was about to pronounce the death sentence. Suddenly, shouts of 'Make way! Make way!' rang out and Frank pushed his way to the front of the court to the astonishment of everyone. The judge demanded to know what he was at and Frank nobly told his story.

'You see before you, my Lord, an unhappy young man who once little thought of violating the laws of his country. I was born a gentleman and bred one. Six months ago I had an easy fortune but an accidental fire reduced me in a moment to beggary.'

He went on to tell the court about his family and how they had all come to Dublin so that he could look for a decent means to procure a subsistence, yet had met only with compliments, bows and frigid politeness but no subsistence.

He described how he had been driven to commit the crime, and how he had promised the merchant that he would not let him be punished for what he (Frank) had done.

'I am guilty,' he said. 'Release this man. I claim his

sentence and demand his bonds.'

The court was by this time in tears. The merchant was released. Frank was condemned and pardoned the very next day and the Lord Lieutenant gave him a place worth £700 per annum. Some time later, the unfortunate merchant who so resembled him died without heirs and left his fortune to Frank Leeson as a reward for his honesty.

An English barrister in an Irish pub in Clifden, Co. Galway commented on the excellence of English laws because they were impartial and English courts were open to all without distinction.

'Huh,' snorted an old fellow in the corner. 'So's the Hilton Hotel in London. If you can pay for your entertainment.'

INTERPRETERS

When the Gaeltacht was really the Gaeltacht, in other words, before it became official, interpreters were employed regularly by the courts. It was not only monolingual witnesses who asked for interpreters because everybody knew that a run-of-the-mill practitioner was no match for an interpreted witness who understood English. The witness had time to frame an appropriate answer to all cross-examination, and one could not be sure of the truth of the interpretation.

Daniel O'Connell once rode in hot and dusty, just in time for the opening of the Cork Assizes. He was waylaid by an old man, who seized him by the boot before he could dismount in front of the courthouse.

'Counsellor,' said the peasant in Gaelic, 'my only boy is on trial for his life and I have only ten guineas in the world. For the love of God and for pity of a poor man, take it and save my boy.'

O'Connell was shocked but he was forced to reply.

'It's kind of you, my friend, to pay me such a compliment, but in truth I do no more than my friends and companions at the bar. By my arrangments with them and the rules of my calling, it is impossible for me to defend the boy, but there are a dozen as good as I am at the game. Give your guineas to James Lyons and I'll stand warrant that the boy will be as well defended as if I appeared for him.'

The old man burst into tears and joined a despondent group that had watched the interview.

When court rose and O'Connell left the building, he saw

across the road a delighted crowd around a handsome youth. Most prominent in the crowd was the old man of the morning. The great advocate strode up and held out his hand.

'The boy is free?'

'He is, thank God.'

'Well, you took my advice and gave your ten guineas to James Lyons.'

'Begor no! I didn't waste it—I gave it to the interpreter.'

An Englishman who was studying Irish attended a court in Kerry in the hope that he might hear some of the old Celtic tongue.

An old lady entered the witness box, obeyed the direction to take the book in her right hand, listened to the words of the oath but, when ordered to kiss the book, proclaimed *'Níl béarla agam.'* (I don't know any English.)

The interpreter had to be found, and had to take an oath (which no one expected him to keep) that he would truly interpret all that the witness might say, whereupon he tendered the Bible to the lady, who eyed it suspiciously and evidenced complete distrust of such observations as the interpreter promulgated in the sweet Irish.

He recited something in the nature of a soliloquy, reinforced by a stirring address that might have roused an army. The old dame then commenced to croon some harrowing tale in a low voice. An interruption from the interpreter, still holding the Bible in his hand, stimulated her to more impassioned speech accompanied by dramatic gestures.

The interpreter uttered sounds like assurances of sympathy and the old crone started another dirge. The English scholar was fascinated, but not so the judge who, after ten minutes, asked not unreasonably, 'What are you talking about? What has she said?'

'Me Lard, she wants her expinses.'

'She must have said more than that.'

'She wants her expinses, me Lard, because her son James had a right to call for her this morning with the car, only the mare have a cut on her leg . . .'

Excited interruption from the lady; excited open-mouthed attention from the young scholar; protest by the interpreter; emphatic dictation by the old lady who knew no English.

Interpreter proceeds: 'I beg your pardon, me Lard. It was not a cut on the leg; it could be the way with her that she could have slipped in the disputed passage.'

'Swear the witness.'

The witness gave tongue again.

'Next witness,' snapped the judge.

The witness immediately snatched the Bible from the interpreter's hand, kissed it with great devotion and, with much nodding of the head and casting of eyes up to heaven, was finally sworn.

Direct examination ran smoothly, but when counsel for the other side rose to cross-examine she gave him 'wan look' and went deaf.

'Do you remember Puck Fair?' was interpreted to her but received no answer.

'I'm warning you, madam,' said the judge, 'you must answer questions or I shall strike out all that you have said.'

This brutal threat provoked a long solo in Gregorian chant, with obbligato by the interpreter followed by a fugue as the lady grew excited. The interpreter got excited, counsel got excited and the Englishman had to reach into his bag for a second notebook.

All the sentiments of humanity and inhumanity might have place in the rising and falling of the woman's tones —tragedy, love, fear, anguish, hope.

'What is she saying?' demanded the judge.

'Me Lard, she says—yes.'

The Englishman reached into his bag again, pulled out his dictionary and frantically riffled through it.

'The fellow's got it wrong,' he wailed. 'There is no such word in Erse.'

An Irishman arrived in the Kenya Crown Colony as a magistrate. The Senior Magistrate explained to him that in the bush things were a bit different from 'home'.

'For example?' asked the new man, Gleeson.

'For example, you will find yourself using an interpreter out here.'

'Sure, we had interpreters all the time in West Cork and a bad lot they were. A hostile witness I can just about stand but a perjured interpreter is the end!'

Gleeson learned to appreciate that there were certain differences between Schull and Narok when one day there was a delay in a case coming to hearing. He inquired as to the reason and received a note from his clerk saying, 'Sir, we need a deaf and dumb interpreter. The accused is dumb.'

———————

Michael McNamara was at one and the same time a practising barrister and the court interpreter from Irish in the courts in which he practised. In spite of the apparent conflict of interest, he administered the oath to defendants in cases where he himself acted for the plaintiff. In one such case the defendant was a debtor.

'Listen carefully now,' said Counsellor Mack in Irish to the defendant, 'to the terms of the oath and repeat them after me: if I do not tell the truth in this case . . .'

'If I do not tell the truth in this case . . .'

'May a murrain seize my cattle . . .'

'What's that, Counsellor? Yerrah, that's not the oath?'

'Go on and repeat your oath: May a murrain seize my cattle . . .'

'Oh, glory be to God! May a murrain seize my cattle . . .'

'May all my sheep be clifted . . .'

'Yerra, Counsellor, what oath is that you're trying to force on me? I never heard the likes of that oath before.'

'Go on, say it. You have to say it: May all my sheep be clifted . . .'

'God have mercy on me soul! May all my sheep be

clifted. Are you sure that's the right oath you're giving me?'

'Get on with it now!'

'May my children get epilepsy . . .'

'Yerra, Counsellor, tell the judge I admit that debt. But will he give me time to pay?'

McNamara was proud of his stratagem. 'Wasn't I right?' he would say. 'What is an oath? Isn't it a calling on God to punish you if you don't tell the truth? And what was I doing but getting that blackguard to tell the truth or face the consequences.'

———————

An interpreter and a witness were having their usual long and heated chat. The judge finally lost patience and thumped the bench.

'Come, come, Joyce, what are you chattering about down there? This is not the place for village gossip. Tell me what the witness is saying.'

'Ah, I wouldn't rightly like to do that, me Lard.'

'You what?'

'He's a foolish ignorant lad, me Lard. I wouldn't like to repeat what he's after saying.'

'This is disgraceful. It's not for you to make such decisions. Do your job, man.'

The interpreter looked sulky.

'If you do not repeat the witness's exact words this very instant, I'll have you committed for contempt of court.'

'He's after asking me "Who's the ould woman up there with the red curtain round her shoulders?"'

IVORY TOWER

The judge who asked 'Who are the Beatles?' may be apocryphal, but Serjeant Sullivan's description of the English barrister's progress from public school to Oxbridge to chambers and, eventually, to the House of Lords, is in danger of acquiring a patina of truth in the Irish Republic. The closed atmosphere of the Law Library can all too easily transform a hothouse into an ivory tower.

One striking example of this phenomenon was the case of the Glenstal-educated judge and the docker from the East Wall who looked like Arnold Schwarzenegger's big brother. The latter had been charged with getting drunk and beating up his wife and two neighbours. He pleaded guilty but his wife and one of the neighbours gave evidence that, except when he had a few pints in him, he was as gentle as a lamb and one could not wish for a nicer husband, father or friend.

The docker's solicitor explained in mitigation that his client had a little weakness, exacerbated by work which induced thirst. Always a quiet, God-fearing man, his tolerance of alcohol was low and unfortunately when he had drink taken his temper was easily aroused, and since he was of unusual size and strength, the consequences were often worse than they would have been if he had been, say, a desk-bound clerk in an insurance office.

Jem was told to stand up. He wore a collarless shirt with a cloth tied round his neck instead of a tie. Around his great waist was a wide leather belt with a thick brass buckle. He wore moleskin trousers and gigantic steel-toed boots. He twisted a coal-smeared cap between his enormous fists.

The judge pronounced sentence.

'My good man,' he said, 'I have heard the testimony of your wife and your neighbour and the eloquent plea by your solicitor and I recognise that yours is an unfortunate case. Drink can be your downfall. You see where it has brought you and, but for a merciful Providence, your case could have been much worse. Serious hurt could have been caused to these good people and where would you be then? Have you thought of that?'

He paused and looked over his spectacles at the giant, who hung his head in shame and contrition.

'I am going to be lenient with you', said the judge. 'I am going to give you a suspended sentence. But . . .and listen to me carefully . . .'

The judge wagged a bony finger at him.

'I want you to give me a solemn promise, here and now, in this court in the presence of your wife and family, that you will never ever touch another drop of alcohol, not even a teeny weeny sherry before dinner!'

An even more extreme case was that of the rather academic and unworldly barrister who emerged from the protected atmosphere of the Law Library to volunteer for service in World War I. One morning in Flanders, a fellow-officer came to Johnston's tent. Outside, convoys of lorries were ploughing through the Flemish mud. All around, men in uniform, with and without helmets, on horses, on motor-cycles, in cars, bellowing, screeching, shooting, digging trenches, were carrying on the business of war. Swarms of angry bullets, hostile as wasps, flew by. In the distance the thunder of heavy artillery was a constant background noise and from time to time a shell would find its target and leave its calling card of smoke, blood, guts and tattered flesh.

Inside the tent, Johnston was seated at a small camp table

covered with papers and books. More papers were on the ground. Moaning and cursing, chewing the end of his pen, Johnston appeared to be shell-shocked. He would pick up letters, scan them and then throw away impatiently.

'What on earth is going on?' asked a friend. 'What's the matter?'

'It's insane, ridiculous,' exclaimed Johnston angrily. 'Just look at this,' and he waved a telegram under the other's nose.

'Here is an order from HQ. They tell me to charge the enemy. I've been through every document in the blessed place. I can find no statements, no complaints. There's not a scintilla of evidence or guidance here to give me any idea of what I am to charge them with, in what court or what jurisdiction!'

———

To the same family belongs the story of the Dublin accountant who bought himself a flashy Porsche. He had to fly to Paris and decided, rather than take a taxi, to drive to Dublin Airport and leave the car there. He left the car in the car-park all right but, absent-mindedly, forgot to take the ticket with him.

When he returned next day, there was no car to be found. It had been stolen. The airport denied liability. They argued that the small print on the tickets stated that cars were parked at owner's risk.

The case went ahead based on negligence and the Law of Contract.

Counsel for the claimant set out to explain to the jury of solid Dubliners what was implied when parties entered into a contract.

'Gentlemen, you have heard a lot of talk today about the Law of Contract and conditions and warranties and implied terms and so many other things that your heads must be spinning. Put all that aside for the moment and think how you yourselves would feel if something like this happened to you. Just imagine it, you drive up to the airport happy and content that you have a nice safe place to leave your motor-car where it will be looked after and cared for just as you would look after and care for something that a neighbour left in your safe-keeping. And this isn't even a question of a neighbour asking you to look after a bicycle or some garden tools, you've paid out good money for a service and you have every right to think that they will look after your property and give it back to you safe and sound. And how would you know that this was what you believed and expected? I'll tell you. By the way you would react if something like this happened to you. Gentlemen, if you were in a similar situation, wouldn't you throw your hands to high heaven and exclaim, "Oh, my goodness gracious me, my sainted aunt. Oh, the villains, they have gone and stolen my shiny new expensive Porsche! These airport people have let it be snatched from under their very noses!" But you would not stop there, oh no, and your very words would disclose what your expectations had been. Wouldn't you tear your hair and cry out, "Oh, dearie me, oh, dearie me, my lovely motor-car has disappeared, my lovely motor has gone"? '

Not only can legal knowledge and vocabulary insulate lawyers from the mundane world of laymen, it provides some with endless food for thought and speculation and, just as soldiers must be unable to appreciate a landscape without evaluating it in terms of terrain, so everything is capable of reminding lawyers of the principles of tort and contract.

Even on vacation the famous Chief Baron Palles thought about the law. During a holiday in France with some friends, one of whom was the recorder of Cork, he went for a walk through the countryside. They had been walking for about an hour, when his companions noticed that he was not with them. They turned back to look for him and found him beside a railway track brooding over an improperly protected railway turntable.

'What are you doing here? What's the matter?'

The Chief Baron looked at the turntable sadly and shook his head.

'Ah, Recorder,' he sighed sorrowfully, 'I'm grieved that they haven't heard of *Cooke* v. *Midland Great Western Railway Company* in this part of France.'

Sir Robert Graham was an excessively polite and considerate judge. Upon one occasion, when passing sentence on a batch of convicted criminals, he absent-mindedly sentenced a man to be transported who was intended to be hanged.

Shocked beyond measure when apprised of his mistake, he ordered the culprit to be placed in the dock again and hastily putting on the black cap, he addressed him.

'Prisoner at the bar, I do beg your pardon . . .' and then proceeded to tell him that he would be hanged by the neck until he was dead.

JUDGES

One of the most honourable and humane judges in Ireland in the eighteenth and nineteenth centuries was Justice Kelly of the Common Pleas. He acquired professionally a great fortune and died at a great age, beloved and regretted by everybody who had known him. He practised several years in the West Indies and, studying at the Temple on his return, was in due season admitted to the Irish bar and rose rapidly.

Towards the end of the eighteenth century, when the Irish insisted on a declaration of their independence, he had attained the high dignity of Prime Serjeant, a law office not known in England. In Ireland the Prime Serjeant had rank and precedence over the Attorney General and Solicitor General. When the government of Ireland opposed the independence of the Irish Parliament, Kelly declared, 'I should rather consider it a disgrace than an honour to wear the Prime Serjeant's gown under a ministry which resisted the rights of my country.'

He immediately sent in his resignation, and retired to the rank of a private barrister. He was an exception.

Kelly was overwhelmingly popular. Nobody was satisfied who had not Tom Kelly for his advocate in the courts. No suitor was content who had not Tom Kelly's opinion as to title. All purchasers of property must have Tom Kelly's sanction for their speculations. He became both an oracle and a fortune-teller. His court bag grew too heavy for his strength, but he got through every cause gallantly and cheerfully, he was always prepared, his arguments seldom failed, his spirits never flagged. He lived splendidly, yet saved a large fortune.

After his appointment to the bench, the public began to find out that his legal knowledge had been overrated; his opinions were overruled, his advice thought scarce worth having, his deductions esteemed illogical. In short, he lost altogether the character of an infallible lawyer, but had the happiness of thinking that he had confirmed his reputation for honour, justice and integrity.

When asked about his legal ability, he had the last laugh: 'So they find out now that I am not a very staunch lawyer. I am heartily glad they did not find it out thirty years ago!'

———————

Lord Norbury was so extravagant in manner that anything might be expected of him and it was not altogether surprising that the nineteenth-century equivalent of The Sun *should run an article claiming that he had appeared on the bench in masquerade dress.*

Jonah Barrington subsequently put the record straight. Some time previously, he wrote, Lady Castlereagh had given a very splendid masquerade, which the Chief Justice attended in the dress and character of Hawthorne in *Love in a Village*, a popular play. The dress was of green tabinet (a watered fabric of silk and wool used for window-curtains and introduced into Ireland by a Huguenot, M. Tabinet), with mother-of-pearl buttons, striped yellow and black waistcoat and buff breeches, and was altogether cool and light.

There was a heat wave when Norbury went on his next circuit and, having a great press of sentences to pass on rebels in Carlow, he put on under his robes the lightest clothes in his wardrobe, i.e. Hawthorne's costume. Now the masquerade dress was a *dead secret* except to the robes that covered it, and neither the passing generations nor the readers of this book of anecdotes would ever have heard a word of the green jacket if the judicial robes had kept themselves close, as the Chief Justice had carefully provided before the sounding of the trumpet.

The warmth of the day, however, and the variety of appropriate addresses necessary to be framed for so many convicted criminals, might be expected to take away a certain quantity of a man's precaution and, as a Chief Justice is still only a man, Lord Norbury fell into the snare and, feeling the heat insufferable, which twisting his wig sideways did not relieve, he involuntarily first turned up the sleeves of his robe, then loosened the zone round his waist. The robe now being free from all restraint thought it had a right to steal away from the green jacket, and Norbury's technicoloured dream clothes were revealed. Everyone in court stared in astonishment but Lord Norbury continued to hear and to sentence, utterly unaware of the picture he presented.

Richard Adams was the judge for the County of Limerick. There were strong elements of the clown in his make-up, but it was buffoonery with brains. No one knew what was going to happen in his court. One day everything was as correct and formal as a textbook court should be. The next day it was a bawdy pantomime.

His decisions were consistently right, his presentation invariably wrong. In the midst of sober and erudite phrases, wild outbursts of scathing wit and surrealistic scatology would erupt. His humour was all too often too broad for the primness of the times and wisecracks too filthy for the smoking room would pepper his pronouncements as it were of their own accord. As a judge he was a good stand-up comic of the Brendan O'Carroll school. He often frightened himself when he read in the newspapers what he had said the day before.

One June evening, Serjeant Sullivan was returning from a successful few hours fishing at Corbally and, as he passed up George's Street, he heard a roar that summoned him across the road to where Adams was standing outside the County Club.

'My God, I'm ruined!' said Adams.

'Well, judge, what has ruined you this time?'

'Have you seen the *Limerick Leader*?'

'I have not.'

'Just look at it.' And he handed Sullivan a copy which contained a report of that day's proceedings in Adams's court. A Limerick bowsey had been prosecuted for an assault on a young woman and there appeared half a column of frank and open discussion between the bench and the dock about the ins and outs of the business, resulting in a dead heat. No punches had been pulled and no Victorian euphemism had been used on either side.

Sullivan handed him back the paper.

'Tell me now, did I say all that?' asked Adams.

'Well, judge, if you call me as a witness I can swear that I did not hear a word of it.'

'Blast you, you were out fishing.'

'I was.'

Adams put on a hangdog look.

'You know, it looks damned like what I do say.'

For some months afterwards, there were dread warnings issued in all the confraternities that young people should keep out of Adams's court.

Nowadays there is a compulsory retirement age for judges. This was not always the case and so, not only were there deaf judges, there were blind ones.

Charles Kelly was County Court judge for Clare and was still on the bench at the age of ninety-one. His calligraphy was beautiful copper-plate but he was incapable of distinguishing the features of the advocates or witnesses who appeared before him. Luckily he had an efficient Clerk of the Crown and Peace called Henry, who prevented court proceedings from turning into chaos.

A visiting QC from Dublin was in Kelly's court one day and noted how Henry kept interfering and correcting the judge.

He turned to his junior. 'I say,' he remarked, 'that Clerk takes a deuce of a lot on himself.'

The junior smiled. 'You should have been here before he was appointed. One day old Kelly insisted on sentencing a man to death for stealing a goat. He declared that there was a special enactment in an ancient Irish statute which forbade the stealing of a goat on pain of death and he could find no trace of any Act of Parliament repealing it, so it must still be law. Luckily, we had the prisoner released the following day and it was either have the bother of trying to get rid of the judge or appointing Henry. Henry got the job.'

Henry knew everybody in County Clare and acted as the judge's eyes and often his conscience too. A case of criminal assault on a young woman had been concluded and the jury had just returned a verdict of Guilty.

'A most proper verdict,' said old Kelly, who had been born and lived in France and retained many of the fashions of the First Empire in dress and manner. 'You are an intolerable young ruffian. Only twenty years old and already committing outrages. You will go to jail for twelve months with hard labour.'

'Six months hard labour,' announced the Clerk of the Crown and Peace.

Judge Kelly might be blind but there was nothing wrong with his hearing.

'Indeed, no, Henry! I said twelve months. It was a very bad case, Henry.'

A wastepaper basket full of apples stood on the registrar's desk. Henry helped himself to an apple. He took a bite, chewed and swallowed.

'All these are bad cases,' he then said. 'But sure he's young and we never give more than six months.'

'I said twelve months and I shall insist on twelve months. I am going to protect girls from young savages like this.'

The clerk of the court wrote something and blotted it.

'Six months with hard labour is what is written in the Crown Book. Take him away.'

'Really, Henry,' the old fellow protested, 'It is wrong to do that. Justice calls for severity. Next time it will be penal servitude.'

'All right,' said Henry, 'perhaps.'

A good prophylactic against being reversed on appeal is for the judge to find as a fact that he does not believe a witness. Since he is the one who has seen the witness perform and has observed his demeanour, it is very hard for appeal judges to override this statement. Obviously, such a finding presented certain (not insuperable) difficulties in the case of Judge Kelly.

A civil case was called before him. The plaintiff came up upon the table and was sworn.

'Who is this, Henry?' inquired his Honour, who was incapable of distinguishing faces at such a distance.

'Plaintiff in number eighty-seven: Mr Mulcahy, one of the most respectable gentlemen in the county. Sure, you know him well.'

'I don't remember him, Henry.'

'Of course, you do. He lives in that nice house where the road branches to Kildysart, and he's on the Grand Jury. Your Honour can trust every word he'll say. He's a very decent man.'

When Mr Mulcahy's solicitor had finished his direct examination, the solicitor for the defendant rose to cross-examine. But Henry had a question for him before he began.

'Who is this you are appearing for, Mr O'Meehan?'

'The defendant.'

'Sure, I know that.'

'Timothy Kelly.'

'Sure, I know that too. I have it in the book. Which Timothy Kelly?'

'He's the little chap from Cloonee.'

'Is he the lad they call "Slant-eye"?'

'The same.'

'The fellow that gave evidence about the goat last sessions.'

'Yes.'

'And he has the impudence to appear here again. All right, go ahead.'

The blind judge found Slant-eye's 'demeanour to be most unsatisfactory' and he was decreed.

Not every judge was as fortunate as Kelly to have a Henry on hand as the following story shows (from Personal Recollections *by Sir Jonah Barrington, 1827):*

Old Judge Henn, a very excellent private character, was dreadfully puzzled on circuit, about 1789, by two pertinacious young barristers, arguing a civil bill upon some trifling subject, repeatedly haranguing the court, and each most positively laying down the 'law of the case' in direct opposition to his adversary's statement thereupon. The judge listened with great attention until both were tired of stating the law and contradicting each other, when they unanimously requested his Lordship to decide the point.

'How, gentlemen,' said Judge Henn, 'can I settle it between you? You, sir, positively say the law is one way, and you,' turning to the opposite party, 'as unequivocally affirm that it is the other way. I wish to God, Billy Harris,' he said to his registrar who sat underneath, 'I knew what the law really was!'

'My Lord,' replied Billy Harris most sententiously, rising at the same moment, and casting a despairing glance towards the bench, 'if I possessed that knowledge, I protest to God I would tell your Lordship with a great deal of pleasure!'

It was alleged that the deafest judge in Ireland presided in the County of

Tipperary. He was walking along the platform of a railway station one day with a member of the bar when they met Carson, who used to practise in the judge's court:

'Good afternoon, judge,' said the newcomer. 'Was there anything interesting in your court today?'

'Eh!' squeaked the judge.

The question was shouted again.

'Oh, yes, my dear Carson! A very interesting case,' the judge replied. 'I'm not quite sure what exactly it was. I think it was a choral society—there was something about the singers disputing about an instrument. I think it was a harmonium.'

Carson could not help but notice that the judge's companion was having extreme difficulty in keeping a straight face.

'What is it, Tom?' he muttered without moving his lips.

'An action for the price of a Singer sewing machine,' was the whispered reply.

Contrary to popular belief, commonsense has been known to override the law. There is an often repeated story about Judge Michael Comyn, whose pride was that he did not leave his commonsense outside the courtroom door.

An action involving the interpretation of a document concerning an agreement for holding cattle was being heard before Michael Comyn. Counsel said that he had obtained an opinion on the meaning of the writing from Mr Arthur Newett, an elderly barrister working in the chancery division.

'Mr Newett,' said the judge, 'Ah, a great man, a great man, very learned in equity matters and in the construction of deeds, leases and wills, no doubt charter parties and bills of exchange, a great man learned in the law.'

Counsel on the other side protested that he had an opinion from Mr Tommy Marnum.

'Ah, a great man too,' remarked the judge, 'an eloquent man and a man who all night pursues lengthy documents of complexity. He knows Coke and every passage in Wolstenholme's Conveyancing.'

The judge paused and looked down at the expectant barristers.

'They know all about the law,' he continued. 'All about deeds and trusts, but I tell ye, gentlemen, I know all about cows.'

In a Workmen's Compensation case, the claimant had suffered an injury to his foot. The justice was the terror of the non-working man. The claimant had been advised that he would have to show his foot to the court and, sure enough, when the time came, he was told to approach the bench, remove his boot and display the injury. This was not enough for the justice. He wanted to see the other foot. The man unlaced his boot and pulled off his sock. The next moment, the court shook to a thunderous bellow.

'How dare you wash one foot only when you come into my court!'

There is a maxim that justice must not only be done but must also be seen to be done. There could also be a maxim that at certain times and places, even a bad decision is better than no decision. Nothing can be more frustrating at times than a judge who cannot make up his mind, particularly as a bad judgement can always be appealed.

Matt Hannon, a District Justice, was a man who worked on the valid legal principle that, where the prosecution has failed to prove its case, the accused is entitled to an acquittal.

Prosecutors, appearing before him, found it rather frustrating that it seemed at times almost impossible to gauge exactly how reasonable the doubt was and that, before giving judgement, the justice would often bow his head in prayer for guidance from the Lord and then say to an old lag, 'Ah, Mister, I have to let you go, because I have a doubt about you, though I have no doubt that my doubt is not the correct one.'

Judge Harrison in Cork Assizes in 1893 went to sleep every day in court. His son acted as his registrar and, in fact, dealt with the cases very competently.

An appeal was brought in the case of a horse bought by a fraudulent claimant. The plaintiff and his witnesses proceeded to give the most elaborate evidence about the horse and his ancestry. The sheriff, however, showed that the horse was addicted to being seized illegally. It had been taken in execution four times but had always belonged to someone else. The bailiff was called to give evidence that the plaintiff had attributed ownership to the last judgement debtor. This bailiff had, in fact, been caught out by Harrison earlier in the day telling untruths. This time counsel deliberately shouted his questions and thumped his desk with his fist until the judge was woken up, at which point counsel started to talk about the morning's case. The bailiff was bursting to talk about the horse but every time that he attempted to do so, counsel interrupted him and brought him back to other matters. Naturally, the judge assumed that he was still hearing the earlier case. The defence was called and claimed that the defendant had nothing to do with the case. Judge Harrison, ruling that he had everything to do with it, gave a decree for £40.

One day in Birr, a plaintiff appeared in court in relation to a dispute over land. When the facts were set out by his counsel, it seemed to be an open and shut case and the defence did little to weaken it. Nevertheless, when it was time for the judge to sum up, he picked so many holes in the plaintiff's case and cast so much doubt on the credibility of both the plaintiff and his witnesses, that the jury had to find for the defence.

That evening at dinner, visiting Queen's Counsel (an old friend) brought up the matter.

'You were a little hard on that poor fellow today, Johny.'

'Do you think so?'

'The facts seemed pretty clear . . .'

'Are you saying that I did not obey the letter of the law and that justice was not done in my court?'

'Well, since you ask, I suppose I am saying just that.'

'Bertie, I plead guilty to the first count but not to the second.'

He cracked a walnut and gesticulated with the nutcrackers.

'When I catch a fellow in my court telling lies, I put him on a blacklist, and for two years, if he comes before me, I decide against him, right or wrong.'

Once upon a time, there were so many Irish judges, magistrates and Crown Counsel scattered throughout the British Empire that the colonial courts could be seen as an extension of the Irish courts. Irish lawyers were much more suited to this sort of work than rarefied London barristers. Anyone who had survived the wiles of Bantry or Bangor Erris would find Sokoto or Bangalore a piece of cake. Pygmies can kill elephants, and peasant skills in derailing the metropolitan juggernaut do not depend on colour or climate and are strikingly similar beside palm, pine or whin bush.

There is a famous story of an Irish magistrate in Fiji whose clerk was always comparing him unfavourably with his predecessor, Mr Hennessy. Mr Hennessy had done this wonderfully and Mr Hennessey had done that one hundred per cent. Hennessy's successor, Seán O'Brien, came to hate the very name of Hennessy.

One day just after the rainy season, the local health authorities discovered pools of water in the magistrate's garden in which mosquitoes were breeding. This was an offence. What should O'Brien do?

He issued a summons against himself and at the next

sitting of his court, read it out and asked if the accused pleaded Guilty or Not Guilty. He then left the bench, went down to the dock and pleaded Guilty.

He returned to the bench and gave the empty dock a stern lecture on the importance of hygiene and public health and the need to obey local ordinances. He then fined himself ten shillings.

Afterwards, very pleased with himself, O'Brien could not help asking his clerk: 'Well, what do you think of that? Do you think Hennessy would have done the same?'

'Oh, no,' said the clerk, 'Mr Hennessy was a strong magistrate. He would have fined himself twenty shillings!'

An Irish judge, Tim O'Leary, was once trying rioters in Nigeria in batches of sixty. He had practised on the old Munster Circuit and had a much less naive view of the probity of the colonial police or their witnesses than had his brothers from Grantham or Tunbridge Wells.

In the cases he was trying the prosecution witnesses were just too confident and definite for his taste. He adjourned for ten minutes and called forward five or six spectators from the body of the court. He ordered them to sit on the ground among the accused. Prosecuting counsel started to protest but one look at O'Leary's face told him it would be pointless.

More witnesses were called and described how people had come in the night with swords and bows and arrows, had set fire to huts and killed livestock and anyone who resisted them. O'Leary asked the witnesses to identify the intruders by going among the prisoners and touching those whom they remembered. As was to be expected, they walked along the lines touching everybody sitting there, including the interlopers who were not on trial.

O'Leary stopped the trial and had all the witnesses charged with perjury.

Law is an art, not an exact science. It is impossible to forecast the outcome of any case; it is a foolish client who demands such a forecast and an even more foolish lawyer who gives it. Certain guidelines can, however, be established. Serjeant Sullivan, who defended Sir Roger Casement in 1916 when he was tried for treason, highlighted the different approaches of different judges to legal matters in a famous comment on the common law courts at the end of the last century:

If you had some merit on your side but thought the law was against you, you issued your writ in the Queen's Bench which was presided over by Mickey Morris, because although Mickey had a good deal of common sense and a great deal of humanity, his ideas of jurisprudence were peculiarly his own.

On the other hand, if you were strongly of the opinion that, however iniquitous your client was, he had the law on his side, you issued your writ in the Court of Exchequer, presided over by Christopher Palles, the greatest judge before whom I ever appeared. Christopher Palles decided according to what he believed to be the law, and would pay no attention to any other consideration that might be advanced before him.

On the other hand there was a third course: if you had neither law nor merits, you went to the Court of Common Pleas, which in that day was presided over by Chief Justice May, before whom no case was certain and no case was hopeless.

Chief Baron Palles was already a judicial legend in his lifetime, but even legends have off-days when their mortality shows through:

Once, he and his best friend on the Irish bench, Lord Morris and Killanin, went to Switzerland together. The Chief Baron brought a good-sized trunk entirely filled with 'yellow backs', the lurid fictions of those days. This was incomprehensible to Morris—'a box full of rubbish', he described it. The 'rubbish' was not opened because the two friends never ceased talking. One day, as they were leaning over a bridge watching the little stream below, the Chief Baron's false teeth fell out of his mouth into the stream.

Overcome with his loss, he sat down speechless on the bank, whilst Morris unlaced his pair of strong boots, took them off and waded in a few inches. Not a sign of the teeth was to be found.

The Chief Baron, a devout Catholic, had already made friends with the village *Curé*, so on their way back to the hotel they stopped to tell him what had happened in case the teeth should be found and brought to him.

The next Sunday, Palles and Morris attended Mass, and as they went along one was silent, for he couldn't talk and the other depressed, since any physical infirmity in others always depressed him. To make matters worse, the *Curé* preached a sermon on the loss suffered by the very distinguished visitor—whom they had with them at the moment in Church—and he suggested that the congregation should turn up after their dinner and all join in looking for the missing teeth. The Church bell rang and out they trooped—and the Chief Baron sat in his room, cross and silent.

'Now is the time for your yellow trash,' said Morris comfortingly as he dragged the trunk in. 'While I am eating dinner, you, my man, can devour these,' and this is what the toothless Chief Baron did for a couple of days until a spare set of teeth reached him from Ireland.

Judges, like ordinary mortals, have their views and opinions on matters like religion, society, morality, the family. It can even get them into hot water when they seem to wander from their purely judicial role and become spokesmen for extreme views of what should or should not be allowed in our society. Other judges have much more balanced views and few were more balanced than the old judge in Athy in the last century who convicted a man of robbing his neighbours.

Counsel for the convicted man made an impassioned speech in mitigation, the gist of which was that the poor fellow had a wife and eleven children and deserved special consideration.

'True, very true,' said the judge, looking over his glasses wisely, 'it is a free country. Nothing can be more proper than that a man should have a wife and a large family; it is his due—as many children as the Lord provides. However,' and he turned his gaze to the prisoner in the dock, 'you have no right, Maguire, even in a free country, to steal your neighbour's property to support them!'

Chief Baron Palles and the Chief Justice, Peter O'Brien, were in Kerry together. The High Sheriff called to their hotel to ask if they wished to drive with an escort to Mass on Sunday. O'Brien, who loved a bit of pomp, was all for it and asked Palles what he thought about it.

'Well, Peter,' said Palles, 'you can make a fool of yourself if you want to, but I'm going to walk.'

Michael Comyn was hearing a Workmen's Compensation case in which the claimant had to prove that the accident which injured him took place when he was engaged in doing something arising out of his employment and not, as the lovely legal phrase has it, while off on a 'frolic of his own'.

The applicant for compensation was a bargee on the Grand Canal and his claim was that he injured himself when he fell off his bicycle. It was his employer's contention that, at the time of the accident (if accident there had been), he should have been on board ship and not jaunting about on a bicycle. The applicant countered that he had been legitimately sent off at the eleventh lock and told to catch up with the barge at the fourteenth lock.

'No way,' said the boss, 'he had no business off that barge at any time that day.'

Michael Comyn took all this in and then put a question to the cyclist. 'Young man, you've been down this way before?'

'Often, my Lord.'

'I seem to remember that there is a public house not far from the canal bank, a tidy place with a thatched roof. Would I be right?'

'You would, my Lord.'

'And I seem to remember that it's run by a widow,' asked the judge.

The young man hesitated. 'It might be.'

'And that she's a young woman.'

'She could be.'

'She is and she's a handsome young woman into the bargain.'

'She could be.'

'Now maybe your bicycle somehow came to a halt there?'

'It might have.'

'I didn't hear you.'

'I might have gone in and had a glass of stout.'

'I see. The widow and the glass of stout.'

Like Sherlock Holmes summing up for Dr Watson, Judge Comyn concluded, 'Gentlemen, sailors are sailors the whole world over.'

A Dublin barman had persistently pressed his unwelcome intentions on a woman in the neighbourhood. He had been frequently sent to prison for it, but prison did not deter him.

The girl had a brother who, on the next occasion of sexual harassment, thumped the offender.

This time it was the brother who was brought before the police court magistrate. The charge was assault.

The magistrate delivered a homily on the impropriety of taking the law into one's own hands, fined the brother sixpence and warned him, 'If the prosecutor annoys your sister again, and you give way to passion and commit the same offence, and are again brought up before me, I will be obliged to double the penalty.'

A judge was once asked to follow decisions given by US and Canadian courts. He was not impressed.

'It used to be said,' he observed, 'that the common law of England resided in the breasts of His Majesty's judges.'

'A very happy residence,' murmured sycophantic counsel.

'But that does not justify exploratory operations,' warned the judge.

The same judge was discussing the measurement of excessive rates of interest charged by Dublin loan-sharks.

There are some people to whom no one would lend anything at any rate of interest whatsoever. In such a case, it would be impossible to say that any amount of interest was unconscionable or extravagant. I think there is an extravagant case put somewhere in the Irish Law Reports. It says: 'Suppose you were asked to lend a mutton chop to a ravenous dog, upon what terms would you lend it?'

In 1857 the government of the day made Mickey Morris recorder of Galway, but his business at the bar in Dublin was considerably interrupted by the sessions he had to hold in Galway and he lost briefs.

One day he was hearing a case where a few pounds were in dispute and the two opposing solicitors argued interminably with great heat. In a few minutes the train for Dublin was due to start. The recorder looked at his watch but the wrangle showed no signs of ending. At last he said,

'See, gentlemen, I must catch the train. Here is the sum in dispute'—throwing down the few pounds as he vanished from court.

———

Morris's besetting characteristics seem to have been impatience and anxiety. He was always nervous about catching trains and equally fussy to get out of them. Lady Gregory told a story of how he and she entered Kingsbridge Station with Morris's head out of the window, calling out as the train passed slowly along the platform:

'Let me out, let me out, I'm locked in with Lady Gregory.'

The guard of the train had locked the carriage door as a compliment to his distinguished passengers.

———

Trains never went fast enough for him either.

'Is it picking mushrooms ye are?' he would shout from his carriage window at the guard or stationmaster at a wayside station if the train delayed too long.

———

Morris had no time for self-importance. Sir Robert Hamilton was appointed Under-Secretary for Ireland and made himself unpopular by endeavouring to cut down salaries while increasing his own.

One night at a Benchers' dinner at the King's Inns, Morris was presiding as Chief Justice and Sir Robert was sitting next to him. In the course of the evening, to the general astonishment, Hamilton said to the Chief Justice: 'I say nothing about your own salary as Chief Justice, but do you not think that the salary of your puisne (lesser) judges is out of all proper proportion to mine, considering the importance and responsibility of my position?'

Morris replied dryly: 'Do you know, Hamilton, that is a train of thought that I think must often pass through the head of my tipstaff.'

Morris did not like the British Treasury either with their constant pin-
pricks and petty economies. Above all, he hated the pompous notes that
they sent out.

Once when Lord Chief Justice, he received a typical letter from the Treasury in London about undue burning of coal in the law courts. Taking one glance at the paper, he threw it into the wastepaper basket, but noted that 'an official from the Treasury, Whitehall, would be calling upon His Lordship that very morning.' He told his tipstaff to send Mrs Maher—the old housekeeper of the Courts—up at once and as Mrs Maher and the British official entered the chamber, the Chief Justice walked out saying, 'Mary, this gentleman has called about the coal.'

In the House of Lords, in a prolonged case over a trade union dispute, Lord Herschell had been interrupting one of the counsel constantly and rather petulantly.

Morris remarked in a loud voice: 'I think we can all understand now from the present proceedings what amounts to molesting a man in his business.'

An action involving a paternity claim was brought before an Irish judge who was seen to be unsympathetic to the claimant from the outset. There was no further doubt about his attitude when he began his summing-up with the words: 'Faking fatherhood is a fruitful field of feminine falsehood.'

A man was being sued on the basis of a hire purchase document which on the face of it appeared straightforward and reasonable but was revealed, as the action developed, to have so much fine print that it looked as if the debtor would barely be left with the shirt on his back.

The judge interrupted the proceedings and turned to the plaintiff's counsel.

'Tell me, Mr McGonagle, when your client issued this hire purchase document, was a magnifying glass supplied with it?'

The same judge was hearing another case involving an alleged breach of contract. The evidence was quite clear, everything in the contract was in favour of the plaintiff. There was nothing in it for the defendant. The judge listened to all the witnesses and then began his address to the jury.

'Gentlemen of the jury, you have heard the evidence in this case as I have and, no doubt, you too will be of the opinion that the contract between the parties was so one-sided that it is surprising that it was written on both sides of the paper.'

A judge in Dublin was fond of a drop and was always sympathetic to an accused when intoxication was pleaded in mitigation. On one occasion, an accused, charged with mistreatment of his family, claimed that on the final occasion he had drink taken and was not responsible for his actions.

Whatever about his earlier behaviour, his actions during the final outburst were so outrageous that not only could the judge find no excuses for him, but he drew sinister conclusions from them.

'If this man remains so bad,' he told the jury, 'even when drunk, what on earth must he be like when he is sober?'

Lord Norbury sat on the bench with Judge Johnson and Judge Fletcher. Norbury was a comedian and his judgements were long, rambling, absurd, comic performances which were the talk of fashionable and sensation-seeking Dublin but drove his brother judges mad. Johnson was a vehement and impetuous man who could not restrain himself whenever his sense of propriety was offended. This was particularly obvious when Norbury was delivering a judgement. Half the fun of the show consisted in observing the reaction of Norbury's judicial partners.

On one such occasion, Fletcher, indignant at the absurdity which was thrown up by Norbury to bespatter the bench, expressed his disgust by an expression of bilious severity which spread over his countenance and grimaced as if he were chewing a particularly bitter lemon. He suffered from an ulcer which had obviously gone into overdrive.

Johnson tried at first to hide his anger and literally thrust his clenched fists into his mouth, but it was clear to the delighted spectators that his indignation was building up to boiling point. After a while, a growl was heard from Judge Fletcher, followed by a groan from Johnson. Norbury ignored both and continued on his merry way.

Judge Fletcher had a habit, when annoyed, of rocking himself in his seat. He was a man of considerable bulk and the swinging which everyone at the bar recognised as a sign of increasing anger would grow more violent as his temper grew. The deeper Norbury plunged into his personal morass of free association, Fletcher's oscillations, accompanied by more bear-like growling, described a greater segment of a circle and shook the whole bench.

Judge Johnson, on the other side of the Chief Justice, his shaggy eyebrows bent and contracted over his face, his eyes flashing with rage, started to blurt out imprecations of indignation and disgust and, from time to time, hurled himself violently around.

In spite of these seismic disturbances on either side of him, Norbury kept going until Fletcher swung round so much on one side that he actually banged into him, and Johnson, throwing his hands up to heaven, hit him on the shoulder on the other side. Norbury then came out of his self-induced trance and gave a start, looking round at the bar, who by this time were punching each other and roaring with laughter simultaneously.

Norbury sized up the situation and discharged two or

three puffs of breath. Then he thanked his brothers for their urbanity and good manners and called on his tipstaff to bring him his chamber pot.

When the pot had been brought to him, he stood up, turned his back on the court and the gentlemen and ladies of Georgian Dublin and noisily pissed on his fellow judges' opinion of his talents.

Of course, at the end of the day, the life of a judge is not an easy one. However independent, judges are still civil servants obliged to cope with tiresome administration and money problems in the seventeenth century as much as the twentieth. Even in those days, barristers complained that they lost money by ascending the bench. The following plea was addressed by Chief Justice Keatinge to the Duke of Ormonde, Lord Lieutenant of Ireland on 28 October 1682:

Mr Justice Turner, having by the two last packets which arrived from London alarmed my brethren the judges that £100 per annum was to be retrenched in the establishment now under consideration from everyone of them out of the allowance made them by His Majesty (James II) for their circuits, they have desired me with all humility to lay the state of the matter before Your Grace and to beg your protection thereon if any such thing be intended, for the scantiness of the allowance as it now stands makes us with reason believe that Mr Justice Turner had been misinformed.

The Lord Chief Justice hath for salary and circuits but £800 per annum, the Chief Baron and judges but £700 and the rest of the justices but £600 and, if any of this should be retrenched, the allowances would not support the judges in any measure to the dignity of the place.

The £200 circuit money was given in lieu of the entertainment formerly given by the judges in their circuits by each Sheriff in his county and of an ancient fee of ten shillings each taken by the Judges of Assize upon every traverse at the assizes both which were then taken from the judges by Act of State in this kingdom nor doth the £200 per annum come altogether in lieu thereof, His Majesty's allowances for robes being likewise part thereof.

Your Grace may be pleased to remember how the office of Sheriff formerly declined by all is now sued for by many competitors in each county for in truth it is become generally an office of great gain and no charge.

The judges have generally long and uncouth journeys with ill and chargeable entertainment and Your Grace found it difficult even as the allowances now stand to get any gentlemen of parts or practice to change the bar for the bench. It will be much more so if the present allowances be retrenched.

JURIES

Jury trials were more free and easy in the nineteenth century than they are today.

One scorching August day in Kanturk two travelling women, young and pretty, were being prosecuted for stealing a roll of banknotes from a cattle dealer. The notes had actually been found in the possession of one of the women when they were arrested. One of the jurors had had a late night and what with the heat of the day and the stuffiness of the court-room he not only fell asleep but slid quietly off the jury bench and rolled under it. Nobody noticed him, the trial proceeded and the two girls were, as usual before a Kanturk jury, acquitted. The jury left, a new jury trooped in and were sworn and a new trial began. The sleeper slept on.

The new case was one of assault. The juror woke in the middle of it, rolled out from under the bench, squeezed in among the newcomers and, refreshed, began to take an interest in the proceedings but, to his dismay, could not understand a word of what was going on. This was not good enough. He raised his hand.

'Me Lard . . .' he called out.

'Hold your tongue, sir', snapped the judge, 'and listen to the evidence.'

'But, me Lard, I want to spake.'

'Well, you can't'.

'But I've not spoken yet.'

The judge was hot and uncomfortable and wanted to go

home. He saw that argument could only delay matters indefinitely.

'This is most irregular. What do you want to say?'

'Me Lard, would you not have the girls go and give the lad back his money?'

The judge now lost his grip. The juror displayed no obvious symptoms of insanity, imbecility or intoxication and was clearly earnest in making his proposal. He leaned over and tapped the bald head of the Clerk of the Crown, who had himself been snatching forty winks in the corner of his seat beside his deputy. To the added horror of the judge, the clerk pronounced the intervention of the juror as not only rational but also helpful.

However, while the judge was trying in vain to make sense of what was going one, the clerk had another look at the jury box. It did not take him long to spot what everyone had missed. There were thirteen jurors crammed into the box. He looked at the dock. The girls had disappeared.

It took even less time to put two and two together and, quick as a flash, he pretended to have misinterpreted the judge's observation and to have understood that the generous juror had returned to the court to make a belated suggestion about the disposal of the money. He indignantly denounced the juror.

'You've been here all the time, you rip you. You've been asleep, haven't you? A mistrial, my Lord, a mistrial. Sleeping in court, begor. He should be held in contempt.'

He then turned on his deputy and tore a strip off him for daring to be negligent while on duty. The juror was ejected and two policemen were sent out to rearrest the two girls before they could spend all the money.

It was always difficult to get jurors in rural Ireland in the last century. Nobody wanted to do jury service and rightly so. Apart from the awkward and embarrassing decisions that might have to be made, poor men often had to walk ten miles or more in all weathers to the assize town to stay there at their own expense for several nights.

On one occasion, just such a reluctant juror pleaded with the judge to excuse him. His Lordship was not sympathetic.

'Why should I excuse you?'

'Me Lord, 'tis a great hardship on me.'

'It's a great hardship on myself but I attend here everyday and do my duty.'

'I'm so old, me Lord.'

'You're ten years younger than I am. I'm very old.'

'I'm deaf, me Lord.'

'I'm deaf too,' snorted his Lordship, 'but I make myself hear.'

'I'm very stupid.'

'And I'm very . . . Now, see here, you've got to serve and that's that. No more nonsense.'

————————

The difficulty of getting jurors was even greater in harvest time, so it was the practice to make the same jurors hear several cases one after another because it might not be possible to round up a new batch. The jurors, anxious to get back to their fields, were up to the court's tricks and their response was to acquit every prisoner without even leaving the jury box to deliberate.

A jury in County Limerick was particularly bad one day and the judge and the Crown Prosecutor were growing desperate. Then the prosecutor realised that there was one juror in the back row who had never taken part in the brief consultations which had preceded each acquittal. He was a dark quiet man who did not look at all like a Limerick farmer.

The prosecutor drew this omission to the judge's attention. The judge raised the matter with the foreman of the jury.

'Why have you never consulted that gentleman in the back row?' he asked.

'Sure, there's no consulting him,' said the foreman. 'He can't understand a word you say. He's a furriner.'

The jury list was consulted and, with extreme difficulty, the man was questioned. It was true that he had not understood a word of the proceedings but he was not a foreigner. He was a British citizen born in the East End of London. He also happened to be a second generation Lithuanian and a Yiddish-speaker with minimal English, who was now settled in Limerick.

His presence posed a nice legal conundrum and put a question mark against the verdict in the previous case and the three that had preceded it. While the impatient jurors looked on incomprehendingly and worried about their crops, bar, bench and court officials mulled over the possibilities. Mr Wasserstein was not a minor, an alien, an ancient, a paralytic, a person mentally or physically too infirm to serve. It just happened that he did not understand the language.

'It's a difficult matter, Mr O'Malley, but I must admit that I am strongly inclined to rule that there is infirmity of mind.'

Mr O'Malley was the solicitor for the defendant and he did not fancy seeing his client in the dock again or risking the perils of pleading *autrefois acquit*, i.e. that, having once been acquitted, he could not be tried again.

'With respect, your Honour, that may not cover the case. Remember Seán Óg Ó Connaire?' (Seán Óg was over seventy.)

'What about Seán Og? What in heaven's name has he got to do with this infernal matter?'

'He is an official interpreter paid to enable your Honour to understand Gaelic-speaking witnesses. If your Honour were to make a ruling that a defect in linguistic training was equivalent to lunacy or imbecility of mind, it might be construed as perverted.'

'Hmm, I see what you mean,' mused the judge. 'That doesn't get us much further does it?'

More discussion until finally the Crown Solicitor, who was possibly a farmer himself, proposed a solution.

'Might I respectfully suggest, your Honour, that while

this passive gentleman has displayed no intelligence whatever, he has displayed just as much intelligent appreciation of today's case as the other eleven, who have ignored every scrap of evidence placed before them. We might as well accept the verdict declared by the foreman.'

And so it was.

_____

When the assizes came to Cork in those days, a long panel of 200 names of possible jurors was called over to record attendances. Many and varied were the demands to be excused. Some were successful, some not:

'Number 21—Thomas O'Brien.'

'Me Lard.'

'Does he answer? Is that the juror?'

'I'm not, me Lard, I'm his son.'

'Where is your father?'

'Sure he have a wakeness in himself.'

'But what's the matter with him?'

'I dinnaw, me Lard, but it could be a blasht.'

'Fined two pounds.'

'Number 57—Timothy Driscoll.'

'Medical certificate, my Lord.'

'Read it.'

'This is to certify that I attended Timothy O'Driscoll this day and found him suffering from contusions upon the lower dorsal region, haemorrhage of the post nasal vessels, and acute echymosis of the dexter orbit.'

'Fined two pounds.'

'Number 93—Daniel Sullivan.'

Letter from the parish priest: 'I attended Daniel Sullivan last night, found him in my opinion dangerously ill and administered the last Sacraments.'

'Excuse him.'

'Number 142—George Nyhane.'

'A letter, my Lord: "My husband George Nyhane died ten years ago, but the rent collector had drink taken and put back his name in the book."'

'Excuse him.'

Bankruptcy was an industry that was at one time largely patronised in Munster. At one trial before the Lord Chief Baron and a special jury, of an action on a promissory note, the learned judge in his summing up adverted to the peculiar circumstances under which the instrument had been given: 'In order that you may understand the legal aspects of this case, it is necessary that I should explain to you, as representing the merchant princes of this city, the meaning and effect of a composition in bankruptcy.'

He was brought to a standstill by something like cheers and laughter in the body of the court, and clear signs of discomfiture in the jury-box.

The foreman and two of his colleagues had just carried off a well-publicised composition in bankruptcy.

An innocent young man with little education was walking out with a young lady who had the elevated position of post-office clerk. The Redemptorists came to town and she started to keep company with a stranger who sold holy pictures, rosaries and scapulars at the Mission stall. The jilted suitor was driven mad by jealousy, fought with the girl and killed her.

The facts were undeniable and defending counsel, Patrick Lindsay, would have a hard fight to get away with a verdict of manslaughter.

He kept his closing remarks to the jury as short as possible and ended them like this: 'Imagine my client's disappointment, his despair, when he didn't meet her in the accustomed place but found her instead in a darkened alleyway with an oily-haired peddler of religious objects in the local mission stalls.

After he sat down, his solicitor whispered to him.

'What were you thinking of? We're done for.'

Lindsay answered. 'Do you ever look at anything? There are five fellow in that jury wearing Trinity ties. A fat lot of time they have for scapulars or missions.'

The verdict was manslaughter.

Patrick Lindsay was appearing for the defence in Castlebar. Feeling that the prosecution had made a very poor showing, he made his closing speech to the jury short and sweet. 'Gentlemen, you do not need to hear my speech in this case to convince you of my client's innocence. You heard the evidence against him, not a tittle tattle of proof is there in this case. I won't waste your time. I merely ask you to acquit him.'

And that was that.

He looked at his watch and decided that he might just have time to snatch a very quick cup of tea before the jury returned with an acquittal. It turned out that he would have had time to drink a reasonable proportion of all the tea in China if he had been so inclined but his thirst for tea declined as hour followed hour and no message came from the courthouse. He cursed his arrogance and stupidity in assuming that he could ever take a case and a jury for granted. Then he cursed the jury for its inability to see something as plain as the dozen noses on their twelve faces. What the hell were they doing when he was cross-examining? He had demolished the prosecution witnesses. A blind cretin could have seen that. Never ever again would he underestimate the idiocy of mankind.

Four hours later, the usher came into the restaurant where Lindsay was sunk in 'loathéd Melancholy, of Cerberus and blackest Midnight born in Stygian cave forlorn'.

'The jury is ready now for Lindsay.'

There were no bones in his legs as he crossed the road and his stomach was heaving.

The jury looked solemn and grim as their verdict was handed to the judge. It was 'Not Guilty'.

A wave of joy washed over Lindsay. He rushed back to his hotel for a whiskey to compensate for what he had been through. Bit by bit, the jury joined him. He congratulated them on their perspicacity. Then, after everyone had had a few pints, he asked the obvious question.

'Mother of God, what were you doing in there? You put

the heart across me. Surely, you saw from the word go that that poor lad never did it?'

The foreman laughed. 'Oh, we knew he was innocent. We settled that in five minutes. But it's how we all know each other but hadn't got together like for twenty-five years or more. Weren't we having a bit of a chat?'

———

There is a natural desire in most citizens to evade jury service where possible. Sometimes, fate steps in to help them. In Mayo some years ago, an employee of the ESB was called up for jury service. He reported to his manager who made alternative arrangements for the week or more that he was likely to be absent. To the manager's surprise, he turned up for work on the afternoon of the day that his jury service was to begin.

'What are you doing here, Christy? Why aren't you over in the court?'

'It's like this. I went over and was sworn in and was made foreman of the jury, no less. It was going to be a good trial. Arson and fraud. Didn't I even know the judge? We were at school together. But he was so wrapped up in his papers and talking to the lawyers that he never noticed me. Then well into the trial, he looked over and spotted me. "Well, hello, Christy, how are ye doing? I haven't seen you for ages."

'The defending barrister had me out of there in five minutes and here I am back to work.'

———

A prime example of the rough and ready advocates of the early nineteenth century was Counsellor Grady. His forte was to make the jury laugh and by his 'hail fellow well met' approach disarm the professional witnesses from the Liberties until he could turn them inside out. His humour had all the logic of Monty Python. Cross-examining a foreign sailor in Limerick, he said, 'You are a Swede, I believe?'

'No, I am not,' the witness replied.

'Well, what are you then?'

'I am a Dane.'

Grady turned to the jury.

'Gentlemen, you hear the equivocating scoundrel. Go down, sir.'

De mediatate linguae, 6. Edward II, a statute which remained in force until 1870, laid down that where a foreigner was arraigned for trial by jury, six members of the jury were required to be aliens but there was no provision that they should be fellow-countrymen of the accused or even of each other. When, as often happened, a Spanish sailor got into trouble in Waterford or Cork, half the jury usually came from Russia, Portugal or Iceland.

In Cork once, the police descended on a French vessel and took away six sailors, who were then empanelled to sit on a jury with six Corkmen. Their ship would be stuck in port until the trial was over. Crown counsel opened his case with an impassioned speech against the accused. He then called his first witness but before the oath was administered, the leader of the six sailors, after an excited conference with his fellows in voluble French, stood up and spoke to the judge: 'Milord, it is not necessaire to call ze witnesses, we accept wiz our 'earts ze assurances of ze Procureur du Roi, ze man is guilty.'

And all six proceeded to climb out of the jury box and head for the open sea.

The unholy fascination of the law is that you win some and you lose some and no one, least of all the judge, can predict the outcome, no matter how much he might wish to.

On one occasion a judge was determined to get a guilty verdict out of a Limerick jury. He knew from experience how difficult this would be and felt that his only hope was to convince them of his leniency. Having resumed the facts in as damning a fashion as he could, he then switched tack and put on his merciful voice.

'You are bound, of course, to convict the prisoner,' he said, 'but don't labour under a misapprehension. No one need assume that this would expose him to a severe sentence.'

He then assumed an expression which said, 'Butter would never melt in my mouth.'

As it happened, in the Limerick courthouse in those days, the barrister's bench had been included in the jury box and the jurors were actually sitting behind counsel for the defence and looking over his shoulder. The latter appeared not to be listening to the judge but to be doodling idly on the back of his brief. Obviously, the front row of jurors could not help but notice that what he had done was, in fact, to write three words. One of the jurors turned to the second row and said, 'About ten years.'

The message was passed on and the accused was duly acquitted.

A case which illustrates the vagaries of juries rather than witnesses concerned a young fellow who had sold some cattle at Kenmare, Co. Kerry.

With money in his pocket, he was chatted up by a woman of the town who fed him one pint too many, got hold of his bundle of notes and went off with them. He soon realised that his money had gone, told the police, who recognising her by his description, went straight to her house. She was sitting in front of the fire and, as they came in, she jolted her lap so as to throw its contents into the fire. But the police were quick enough to grab the contents, which turned out to be banknotes. The purchaser of the boy's cattle subsequently identified them as the notes that he had paid over. It seemed to be an open and shut case but the jury found her not guilty of larceny. Perhaps they had had the odd pint with her themselves.

Her solicitor immediately asked that the money be given

back to her. The judge agreed but the jury was to a man upset and the foreman protested.

'Your Honour, it was the intention of the jury that the girl should go free all right, but we all think the boy should have his money back.'

———

In the emotional atmosphere of a lower court, the effect of a charge on a jury is very different from that obtained when it is dissected logically in the hygienic surroundings of a Court of Appeal.

A barrister, acting for a close friend, took the unusual step of showing the friend, his client, the text of the speech which he had prepared to deliver in the latter's cause. The client, having studied it, told him that he read the speech once and felt his cause to be impregnable; upon a second reading, he was not quite so satisfied with it; but having read it for a third time, he thought his cause already lost.

The barrister replied: 'The jury will hear it only once, Mick.'

———

A defendant in a libel case had a certain moral justification for what he wrote about the plaintiff. The plaintiff's expensive senior counsel had convinced the jury otherwise.

Leaving the court-room, the defendant threw a penny to the plaintiff and told him, 'Here, take your character out of that and give me the change.'

———

A pupil barrister or 'devil' asked her master, 'What's the best way to deal with juries?'

'First butter them up and then slither them down,' was the answer.

———

A more direct way was that of the Irish colonel of dragoons, who being informed by his counsel that if there was anyone in the jury to whom he had personal objections, he could legally challenge them. He immediately declared, 'Faith and so I will! If they do not bring me off handsomely, I'll challenge every man jack of them!'

Their rightful place:

As a judge was entering the court in Tuam in 1904, the crier called out to the members of the jury waiting in the court below: 'Gentlemen, please take your places.'
Every one of them walked into the dock.

LANGUAGE

The Queen's English is not the only language in which legal actions have been conducted in Ireland. Gaelic, Latin, Norman-French and plain old Hiberno-English have all had their day and often, whenever their paths crossed, a story was born.

Lord Redesdale (an English judge who was parachuted into Ireland) found the change of linguistic climate baffling. A cause was argued in chancery in which the plaintiff prayed that the defendant should be restrained from suing him on certain bills of exchange, since they were nothing but 'kites'. (To fly a kite is to raise money by issuing an accommodation bill.)

'Kites?' exclaimed Lord Redesdale, 'kites, Mr Plunkett? Kites never could amount to the value of those securites! I don't understand this statement at all, Mr Plunkett.'

'It is not to be expected that you should, my Lord,' answered Plunkett. 'In England and in Ireland, kites are quite different things. In England the wind raises the kites, but in Ireland the kites raise the wind.'

'I do not feel any way better informed, Mr Plunkett,' said the matter-of-fact Chancellor.

'Well, my Lord, I'll explain the thing without mentioning those birds of prey.'

At dinner one evening, Redesdale, having failed to carry on an amusing conversation with Mr Serjeant Toler, and determined to say a civil thing or two, turned to Mr Garrat O'Farrell, a jolly barrister, who always carried a parcel of coarse national humour about with him.

O'Farrel was a broad, squat, ruddy-faced fellow, with a great aquiline nose and a humorous eye. Independent in mind and property, he generally said whatever came uppermost to his mind.

'Mr Garrat O'Farrell,' said the Chancellor solemnly, 'I believe your name and family were very respectable and numerous in County Wicklow. I think I was introduced to several of them during my late tour there.'

'Yes, my Lord,' said O'Farrell, 'we were very numerous; but so many of us have been lately hanged for sheep-stealing that the name is getting rather scarce in that county.'

A ship called the *Memphis* had struck on the Kedges off West Cork, in a hurricane. From the shore came rescuers from Sherrin, Baltimore, Barloge and the islands. With incredible skill and bravery, the crew were saved, landed and hurried off inland while the heroes proceeded to collect their reward. Back they went to the ship and relieved her of her cargo and contents in accordance with the law of the coast.

Prosecutions followed, to the great indignation of all West Cork.

One old longshoreman, when arraigned for larceny and receiving, replied, 'Sure, I'm guilty, me Lard, but I did not know there was any wrong in it.'

'I understand the prisoner has pleaded guilty,' said the Crown Prosecutor.

'He did not,' said the Chief Baron. 'He said he did not have the *animus furandi*,' (i.e. the intent to steal).

'Indeed, me Lard, I did not,' said the accused, 'only an oul' lifebelt, a couple of oars and a small keg.'

Paddy Flemming, a master of Hiberno-English, appeared for the plaintiff in an action for slander at the turn of the century. His client had been described as a 'crow pratie picker'.

'What on earth is slanderous in that, Mr Flemming?' asked the judge. 'It sounds to me like mere vulgar abuse, colourful though the imagery may be.'

'Gor, not at all, your Lordship, 'tis the worst kind of accusation. If your Lordship now was turning out the potatoes in the ridges with a riser, the crows would follow your Lordship's track and pick up the tiny potatoes at the end of the stalk. A crow pratie picker is a mean thief.'

Flemming went on to develop evidence of malicious intent.

'In his affidavit to remit this case, my Lord, the defendant swore that my client was a widow woman, whereas the real truth is that she's quite d'opposite.'

'Would you mind telling me, Mr Flemming, what is the opposite of a widow?'

'She's not a widow.'

Paddy Flemming was born in the Galtees in County Tipperary and spoke a type of English that became known at the bar as Paddy Flemmish.

'Gor man,' he used said to a dull colleague, 'how's your uncle? I heard that he'd a like to die.'

'Well,' was the reply, 'the old gentleman is better. He was quite resigned to the idea of death, but he did not express any desire for it.'

'I didn't mean that,' said Paddy, 'but that he'd a like to die.'

An old lady, having been knocked down at a crossing, sued the driver of the pony trap that had collided with her. The driver said that something had caused the pony to bolt and he called a young constable as a witness.

'The way it was, your Honour,' said the constable, 'whin the pony come to the crossin' dere was a low wall on d'right-hand side belongin' to Flaherty's, an' inside in d'garden behind d'wall, your Honour, Mrs Flaherty had hung up some female garments on a line. I couldn't tell you now what dey were, but dey were garments of some sort, your Honour, and whin d'pony come round he just pricked up his ears an' he looked at thim, and thin the wind blew thim into all sorts of quare shapes, an' d'pony because he couldn't make thim out at all at all, he tuk fright.'

'Yes,' said Judge Adams, 'there is something about that in Tacitus: *Omne ignotum pro magnifico.*'

'Your Honour took d'words out of me mouth,' said the constable.

The tendency of lawyers to make use of an ornate English vocabulary has often given rise to misunderstanding in court.

On one occasion a prisoner was chewing tobacco while in the box.

The justice was growing more and more irritated.

'See here,' he told the accused, 'you must really stop masticating in court.'

Again the reply was a blank and incomprehending 'Wha'?'

'Do stop masticating.'

'Uh, wha'?'

The justice signalled to a police officer. 'Explain to him, for goodness sake.'

'Take your hands out of your pockets,' said the Sergeant.

Leslie Foster was rumoured, by those who did not like him, to be, if not the President of the Royal Academy of Laputa or the father of Martinus Scriblerus, the reincarnation of the professor at Bruges who challenged all mankind to dispute with him *de omni rescibili et de quolibet ente.* And the following story was told in the Law Library whenever Foster's name came up in conversation.

Sir Thomas More, another lawyer, was visiting Bruges in 1530 when an arrogant fellow set up a challenge that he would answer any question that could be propounded to him.

Sir Thomas immediately asked him—'Are cattle taken in withernam irrepleviable?'—adding that one of the ambassador's retinue was ready to dispute with him.

The arrogant challenger was 'gravelled'.

———

Like all gentlemen of the old school, Sir John Chute Neligan liked to embellish his remarks with appropriate Latin tags. The cases for the great Southern Railway Company were being handled by a man called Alfie Blake, who had not had the benefit of a classical education. One day in East Cork, a railway case came to an end and Alfie sat back, pen in hand, waiting to record upon the process the decision of his Honour.

Sir John treated the court to ten minutes of Cicero. Silence followed to be broken by Alfie, who asked the recorder politely, 'I beg your Honour's pardon but would your Honour mind giving us the small change of that in the English language.'

Alfie marked his process DWP, 'dismiss without prejudice', and left the court.

The next case was not ready to go on and was postponed.

'The court will now adjourn,' said Sir John, *'de die in diem.'*

He paused and looked around the court.

'De die in diem. Since I am not asked to translate it, I presume that there are now none but educated gentlemen present.'

———

Serjeant Sullivan is credited with a famous 'spake' which has passed into everday speech. He himself credits it to

Henry Harte Barry, the doyen of Kanturk.

Barry was appearing before Sir John, when the recorder asked him, 'Mr Barry, has your client never heard *Sic utere tuo ut alienum non laedas?*'

'Not a day passes, your Honour, on which he does not hear it. It is the sole topic of conversation where he lives at the top of Mushera mountain.'

Usage of language can divide people of the same country and in court can frequently give rise to misunderstanding.

Counsel for the prosecution was examining one of his own witnesses in Monaghan in the 1950s.

'Mr McCrudden, are you a friend of the accused, Owen Hanratty?'

'No, Your Honour, I'm no frien' of his.'

'What's this? You aren't his friend?'

'No, sir. I was never a frien' of his.'

Counsel saw a vital element of his case disappearing down the drain.

'Are you saying in this court that you are not a friend of Owen Hanratty?'

'I am.'

'Weren't you at school together? Didn't you play football together? Usen't you lend him your horse?'

'I did.'

'But you're not a friend of his?'

'I am not.'

Counsel looked distressed. The judge peered at him inquiringly.

'Yes, Mr Gibson?'

'This is most unusual, my Lord.'

'Do you wish to treat this witness as hostile?'

'I may have to, my Lord.'

The judge took a hand in the proceedings.

'Mr McCrudden, are you an enemy of Mr Hanratty's?'

'Oh God, no, your Honour. I like him well.'

'But you're not his friend?'

McCrudden shook his head.

At this point, a local solicitor who had been trying in vain to attract someone's attention, stood up.

'My Lord, if I might be of help . . .'

'Yes, Mr Martin?'

'In this part of the country, a 'friend' is a blood relative. Mr McCrudden is only saying that he is not related to Mr Hanratty!'

During World War I such a misunderstanding almost turned out to be fatal.

An English general, with a quick temper, was passing his headquarters one morning in 1918 and as the guard turned out, his eye caught something that needed attention. He was irritated by it and turned on the unfortunate corporal and growled: 'Didn't I tell you last week to correct that?'

The corporal, from the mountains of Tyrone, replied meekly, 'I don't mind you telling me, sir.'

The general was in danger of apoplexy. He ordered the corporal to be arrested and swore that he'd teach him to mind the command of a field officer. There was a serious risk that Austin Maguire would be shot.

The Irish officers, when they heard what had happened, gave the general time to cool down and, that evening, diplomatically let it be understood by their superior that, when a Tyrone man says he does not 'mind' something, he means that he does not remember it.

Use of vernacular speech can have different effects on different people. A Dubliner was charged with beating up a girl whom he met at a dance in Parnell Square. His counsel decided that the best form of defence for his client was attack. 'Come on now, aren't you just telling a tissue of lies with this all talk of beating? This man never raised his hand to you that night but you, on the contrary, gave him an almighty dunt in the bollocks.'

The District Justice sat up instantly.

'What did you say, Mr Morton?'

'I said that she gave him a dunt in the bollocks.'

'I'm not familiar with that word.'

'Bollocks? I apologise, your Honour, I was using the only type of language that a witness like this would understand. It means "testicles".'

'Everyone knows that. It's the other one that puzzles me. What on earth does "dunt" mean?'

———

Phrases and vocabulary which might do very well in Court No. 4 or in the Horseshoe Bar in the Shelbourne Hotel do not always fit the bill in Ballyporeen.

Once a barrister called Kinahan was cross-examining a witness in what to him was the clearest of clear language and most obvious terminology.

'Having regard to the *locus in quo*,' i.e. the place where the accident or crime occurred, he asked the witness, 'will you kindly demonstrate to his Lordship the point of impact.'

The witness did nothing. He looked at the barrister. He looked at the judge, Chief Baron Palles. He chewed his lower lip and adopted an expression of sullen fear.

Kinahan was just about to tear into the unfortunate for his unwillingness to answer when Palles came to the witness's rescue.

'See, see, Mr Kinahan,' he interrupted, 'just ask the man where he was hit.'

———

A very junior barrister had been suddenly abandoned by his leader in the middle of an extremely complicated case involving the law against perpetuities, entails, inheritance and a wicked uncle who was the guardian of his client. As he struggled through the mass of old documents, he became more and muddled and kept repeating to his Lordship, like an incantation, the Norman French phrase '*En ventre sa mère*', 'In his mother's womb'.

The judge stopped him.

'Mr Nugent, what is all this about *en ventre sa mère*?'

Counsel on the other side cut in and suggested suavely, 'My learned friend is surely referring to the applicant's uncle. Perhaps he means *in loco parentis*?'

In a case for a non-suit in an ejectment on grounds of extreme technicality, the young Christopher Palles, later to be known as one of the most learned common lawyers in Ireland's history, was opposed by a barrister, Francis MacDonagh, whose knowledge of the law was said to be slight, and the latter kept on decrying 'his learned young friend'.

Palles won his point before the ancient Chief Justice Lefroy, who that evening was heard to remark, 'Horace for once is wrong, *"proximos illi non occupavit Palles honores."*' (Horace had asserted that 'the place nearest in honour to that of (Zeus) belongs to Pallas, brave in battle.' Odes I. XII. 20)

LAW AND POLITICS

Politics and law have always been intimate in Ireland. Before the arrival of the publicans, auctioneers and national school teachers, lawyers appear to have dominated the Irish legislature. Before the Union, barristers and the landed gentry were the tribunes of the people ('people' being very selectively defined). Since the establishment of the common law system, the right of way to the bench often crossed the floor of the house in College Green and Westminster.

While revolution was raging in France, a clergyman, the Rev. William Jackson returned to Ireland from Paris to organise another revolution here. He was arrested, tried and found guilty of high treason in corresponding with the enemy in France.

He was brought up to receive sentence and it was obvious that he was badly affected by what was about to happen. His limbs seemed to totter and large drops of perspiration rolled down his face. In spite of his cloth, he was obviously in a state of abject terror at the prospect of the death sentence.

The judge began his usual little sermon before pronouncing the sentence, but the prisoner seemed to pay little attention to the lecture, being concerned with his own preoccupations. He covered his face and seemed about to faint. The judge paused, the crowd expressed surprise at the poor showing the prisoner was making. The latter continued to droop and, finally, his limbs giving way, he fell down in the dock.

A physician was summoned, examined him and announced that it was too late. Jackson was dead. Before coming into court, he had taken a large quantity of arsenic and aquaforte mixed in tea. No judgement was pronounced against him. He had a splendid funeral which to the astonishment of Dublin was attended by several members of parliament and barristers—including a Counsellor Richard Guinness.

It being observed by some member that the Serjeant-at-arms should have stopped an intruder at the back door of the Irish House of Commons, Sir Boyle Roche very justly asked the honourable gentleman, 'How could the Serjeant-at-arms stop him in the rear while he was catching him at the front? Do you think the Serjeant-at-arms could be, like a bird, in two places at once?'

There once was a particularly annoying, but well connected, solicitor who was chairman of a political committee in County Offaly. He had refused to attend a particular meeting and his colleagues were deciding how to deal with the situation.

'I think we should insist that he comes along and let him know exactly what we think of him and the whole situation,' suggested one hot-headed young solicitor.

'There's no need for that,' said an older man. 'Let's just hold the meeting without him and laugh in his face behind his back.'

Another tale from Barrington:

There once was a barrister called Egan who was one of the roughest-looking persons possible. He was a supporter of the government and spent much of his time in the Irish House of Commons railing against the French Revolution. His figure was coarse and bloated and his dress not over-elegant. In fact, he looked more like a *sans-culotte* or revolutionary than an honourable member of the Irish parliament.

Annoyed one evening by a speech of Henry Grattan's, he declared that the right honourable gentleman's speech had a tendency to introduce the guillotine right into the very body of the House; indeed, he almost thought he could perceive it before him.

Grattan replied that the honourable member must have a vastly sharper sight than he had. He certainly could not see such a thing.

'But though,' he added, looking with his glass towards Egan, 'I may not see the guillotine, yet methinks I can perceive the executioner.'

Irish Catholics had a wonderful opinion of Edmund Burke's assistance and abilities and, because he was a clever man, they thought that his son must be equally talented. He was paid £2,000 to come to Ireland to superintend the progress of their Emancipation Bills in the Irish Parliament shortly before it was swept away by the Union. The Bills were introduced and resisted. Young Burke prepared a petition and, since it was neither well-timed nor well-prepared, many even of the most militant Catholics refused to present it.

The young man, either because he was ignorant of parliamentary rules or because he thought Ireland was the sort of country where you could get away with anything, particularly if you were the son of the great Burke, decided to present the petition himself, not at the bar, but in the body of the House!

He came down from the gallery and walked into the House and up to the Treasury bench with a long roll of parchment under his arm. Very few present had any idea who he was. The result was pandemonium. Shouts of

'Privilege! A stranger in the House!'; calls for the Serjeant-at-arms to do his duty; the serjeant running about with a drawn sword. Burke ran and, after a chase round the chamber, managed to force his way through the enemy behind the speaker's chair and escape.

Messengers were sent to arrest him. This time it was Lord Norbury who defused the situation. Someone observed that no such thing had ever happened before and Norbury exclaimed, 'I found the very same incident some days back in the cross readings of the columns of a newspaper. "Yesterday a petition was presented to the House of Commons, it fortunately missed fire, and the villain ran off."'

The laughter that followed put the House into good humour. Master Burke went back to England with his tail between his legs.

In 1957, the coalition government lost an election. John A. Costello, James Dillon and Patrick Lindsay drove to Áras an Uachtaráin to hand back their seals of office (or, as Lindsay called them, their sodality medals). All three were barristers, although Dillon never practised. They drove down the Quays on what was then the McBirney's side and passed the old Irish House, a public house which often features in photographs of old Dublin.

James Dillon said, 'You know, I never fail to be intrigued by that old Irish House.'

'If you saw it four times a day coming from the Four Courts,' said Costello, 'you wouldn't be a bit impressed.'

The conversation continued with Dillon saying, 'You know I was never in a public house in my life, except my own in Ballaghdereen, which I sold, because when I saw people going home having spent so much money on drink, I decided that they were depriving their families of the essentials.'

Then, to Lindsay's consternation, Costello said that he was in a public house only once in his life, in Terenure, and was nearly choked by a bottle of orange.

Lindsay was appalled and exclaimed, 'Holy Mother of Jaysus, I now know why we are going in this direction today and why we are out of touch with the people.'

John Mitchel was imprisoned in Van Diemen's Land for forty-eight hours because of a misunderstanding over his papers. This is his reaction:

The police magistrate, I suppose, could not have acted otherwise; a want of papers and passports is certainly suspicious; and contemptuous behaviour irritating to the magisterial mind; at any rate the affair was wholly indifferent to me but for one circumstance —my wife might arrive that very day . . .

But for this chance I would have regarded my imprisonment as a wholesome and tonic mental medicine. There is a danger of us growing too soft, good-humoured and balmy, in our present bush life, breathing an air so luxurious, and seeing the face of no present gaoler; therefore, to hear the wards occasionally grating in a British lock I regard as a salutary stimulant, and think of taking a course of it once a year while I remain in captivity.

In 1887 a new Crimes Act was passed which gave the Lord Lieutenant power to 'proclaim any association as dangerous and suppress it', provided for trial without jury and compelled witnesses to give evidence, even though it might incriminate them.

Edward Carson was appointed counsel to the Attorney General, or 'Attorney's Devil', and over the next four years earned himself the nickname 'Coercion Carson'.

The first case he prosecuted was a very famous one arising out of a riot in Mitchelstown, Co. Cork. Gladstone's phrase 'Remember Mitchelstown' was to become a Home

Rule battle-cry.

Carson slept in Fermoy the night before the trial because local feeling was such that it was impossible for the Crown counsel to obtain accommodation at any inn in Mitchelstown. He drove over early in the morning and, on approaching the town, saw that the roads and lanes were dense with people on their way to a mass meeting. Many of them were on horseback and all were armed with heavy sticks. The jaunting-car-driver became understandably alarmed.

'This is a dangerous business, Mr Carson,' he said. 'Do you mind if I throw up my cap and say "Three cheers for William O'Brien"?'

'Not in the least,' replied Carson.

The driver did so and they got through.

During a subsequent trial, following an adjournment, William O'Brien was removed to the nearby jail where he spent the evening singing patriotic songs with his fellow prisoners so loudly that the jailer was obliged to come in and caution them.

'Gentlemen, I don't wish to interfere with your diversions, but there is an echo in this place and I'm afraid that you'll be heard by them bloody Bobbies outside.'

A story, which is not so very funny today, is told of serious rioting in Belfast in 1886 inflamed by the opportunistic rhetoric of Lord Randolph Churchill. The following evidence was given at a trial following one such riot:

A rioter had caught a policeman, held his head down and proceeded to batter him. Presently a second rioter appeared on the scene.

'What have you there, lad?'

'A policeman.'

'Hold on and let me have a thump at him.'

'Get along out of that,' shouted the first rioter between thumps. 'Go off and find your own policeman.'

———————

Mr Serjeant Toler (later Lord Norbury) went as judge on the first circuit that Jonah Barrington went on in 1788 as barrister and the latter considered that they were friends. One evening, however, Toler came into the Irish House of Commons after a boozy dinner with Lord Clare (Barrington's declared enemy) and insulted Barrington in the House. Although Barrington himself had had a few drinks that evening, he limited himself, because of their supposed friendship and because Toler was normally good-tempered, to remarking: 'I shall give Mr Serjeant Toler only that character which developed itself by his versatility —namely, that he has a hand for every man and a heart for nobody.'

The sarcasm struck home. Toler gave back a very 'warm' answer, gave Barrington 'the wink', and made his exit. Barrington had been challenged and, of course, followed.

The Speaker instantly sent the Serjeant-at-arms to pursue the pair with his attendants and bring them back to the House. Toler was caught by the skirts of his coat fastening in a door, and they laid hold of him just as the skirts were torn off. Barrington was overtaken, whilst running away, in Nassau Street and as he resisted was, to the admiration of the mob, brought back like a sack across the shoulders of one of the attendants and thrown down on the floor of the House.

The Speaker told them that they must give their words of honour forthwith that the matter should proceed no further. Toler got up to defend himself, but having no skirts to his coat, cut a ridiculous figure. It was John Philpot Curran who saved the situation. He stood up and with a perfectly straight face declared: 'Mr Speaker, this is the most unparalleled insult that has ever been offered to the House! It appears that one honourable member has trimmed another honourable member's jacket within these walls and nearly within view of the Speaker!'

He brought the House down.

Before the Parnellite split, it was not considered good form for a defeated candidate to lodge a petition against his opponent on the grounds of treating, i.e. the corrupt practice of paying for the conveyance of voters to the polls. After the split it became a good source of income for lawyers.

A moderate amount of rioting and intimidation was another matter. Serjeant Sullivan was trained by one Dr Tanner MD, MP in the art of election rioting. Tanner was rarely sober and his conduct in the House of Commons was extremely embarrassing to his newly respectable colleagues in the Irish Party.

'That fellow Tanner,' Parnell said one day to a group of the party, 'is out there in the lobby declaring that he is about to commit suicide. Can none of you fellows persuade him to do it?'

Rows over important jobs have been known to bring down governments, but 'important' is a relative term.

The Petty Sessions Clerk of Schull, Goleen and Ballydehob, Co. Cork earned less than fifty pounds a year, but even that job was worth fighting for.

When the justices for the United Petty Sessions of Schull, Goleen and Ballydehob met for the first time to elect a clerk, the result was a tie.

The court of King's Bench held that one magistrate was not qualified to vote. The election was quashed.

A second election was held. This time the election was quashed because the chairman of some council, an *ex officio* magistrate, had failed to make a proper declaration on the assumption of a judicial office.

A third election took place. Two magistrates, who would have turned the scales against the successful candidate, had failed to appear for the election. Why had they not appeared? Their names had turned up on the lists of those entitled to vote, but investigation had shown that both were very old men who had left the county years before. One had retired to the Isle of Wight, the other was living in Donegal.

The friends of candidate A went to see both gentlemen and persuaded them to return on an all expenses paid holiday to south-west Cork. The money was thrown away. The friends of candidate B got wind of what was happening and, in the case of the Donegal man, pretended to be agents of the original negotiator and gave him such wrong instructions that he ended up in Tralee, Co. Kerry.

When the gentleman from the Isle of Wight landed in Ireland, he was received by persons whom he took for candidate A's party, who welcomed him and entertained him. Too well. His affidavit declared that, from half-past ten of the morning on which he arrived and had been brought to a hotel to rest himself, until half-past five the next morning when a steward opened his cabin door and told him that the ship was approaching Fishguard, there was a complete blank in his memory and, he believed, in his consciousness.

Free trips to the south coast and abduction of magistrates were held not to be in accordance with the spirit of the Petty Sessions Act, so for the third time one of the great prerogative writs was issued to supply a properly qualified Petty Sessions Clerk, elected by the properly qualified justices of the united districts of Schull, Goleen and Ballydehob.

In Cork in 1868 a Fenian was being tried and the Attorney General had blundered by putting into evidence the complete file of a Fenian newspaper. The accused, having some sense of humour, protested that this evidence against him should be fully and accurately conveyed to the jury, and suggested that it was the duty of the Attorney General to read the whole of the exhibit instead of picking and choosing any phrase or sentence which would suit his case.

A fair and sensible judge would have told the Attorney General to read and enter as evidence only those parts of the publication upon which the prosecution relied. The presiding judge in this case, Keogh, was neither fair nor sensible. He told the prisoner that he would have to read the file himself, commencing at issue number one, page one, column one. The accused did so until lunchtime and then asked for an adjournment for lunch. Keogh refused, but gave permission to everybody else in court to refresh themselves. The same thing happened at dinnertime. Keogh dined and took his supper on the bench while his victim read on.

At three o'clock in the morning the prisoner collapsed exhausted and, in a few minutes, was sentenced by the sneering judge.

Keogh had, in fact, been elected as the spokesman of the Irish Republican Brotherhood but, immediately on election, had gone over to the government and received his reward.

These lines were written about him:

> Capricious Goddess who by pitch and toss
> Doth still award the diadem and cross
> What different fates await the Fenians here
> The fools that are so and the rogues that were.
> The felon's dock awaits O'Leary so
> The seat of judgement is the seat of Keogh;
> Thrice happy Keogh who if he's not belied
> Now tries the crimes for which he was not tried
> And seated on the bench doth safely mock
> The nobler felon standing in the dock.

Lord Peter O'Brien of Kilfenora (Pether the Packer) may have been an opportunistic Tory but he recognised the realities of legal/political life.

Some time after his Unionist conversion had elevated him to the rank of Chief Justice, he was dining with a nationalist barrister who warned him, 'I'm taking the chair at a League meeting next Sunday and you mustn't mind if I take a belt at you.'

'Belt away, Pat,' replied O'Brien.

The very narrow viewpoint which sees the universe in terms of the courts and their procedures can extend to politics and law.

In the last century, it was compulsory for a barrister to become a Member of Parliament before he could become Attorney General or Solicitor General on his upward journey to the bench, even though he might have had no previous interest in or experience of political life.

One such person was Samuel Walker, who was obliged to take his seat in the House of Commons on becoming Solicitor General in 1884. He had never strayed far, physically or mentally, from the Law Library or the Four Courts and was a genuine innocent abroad in the Mother of Parliaments. The poor fellow was horrified by the first debate that he attended and, when asked afterwards what he thought about it, spluttered in incredulous dismay, 'Well, I could hardly believe my ears. I heard men on either side of the House making the most material statements without even a scrap of an affidavit to support them!'

For too long in Irish history, political causes gave work to the courts and influenced their decisions. At certain times, this was more obvious than at others. One such time was 'the Troubles'.

The conduct of a court martial in 1919 was so disgraceful one day that Michael Comyn threw his brief down on the table and said angrily to the court, 'Shoot them if you like, but at least try them first.'

Under the Treaty of 1921, there existed a right of appeal to the Judicial Committee of the Privy Council, which could decide in the last instance on all actions brought before Irish or dominion courts. Two English-born civil servants, Wigg and Cochrane, were dissatisfied with the amount of retirement compensation awarded them by the Irish Supreme Court and lodged such an appeal.

John A. Costello, then Attorney General, and Victor Bewley duly appeared at Number 11 Downing Street to contest a preliminary application for leave to appeal on behalf of the civil servants.

The solemn character of the surroundings, the knowledge that next door to them stood the British Prime Minister's residence where so many decisions had been taken which had altered the history of the world, the majestic and silent servitors, the combined air of learning and tradition which seemed to invest the building—all this taken together was not without an intimidatory effect on Bewley. He could not entirely suppress the illogical fear that their Lordships would approach the case from some angle undreamed of by Costello and himself, or produce from the stores of their accumulated legal knowledge some precedent which the Irish lawyers had overlooked.

Their Lordships took their seats, Costello and Bewley were called in, the arguments began. What impressed Bewley, however, more than the argumentation, was the fact that the highest judicial authorities of the British Empire obviously knew very little of the Pensions Acts and nothing whatever of the various laws and orders governing the relations between Britain and Ireland, and that they had not taken the trouble to familiarise themselves with them before the hearing. The questions which they addressed to counsel did not betray a high degree of legal acumen; from time to time one or the other would make an amiable little joke. One had the impression that the whole affair was to them of supreme unimportance.

When the hearing was over, Bewley and Costello walked down Whitehall with Costello. 'Do you know the average age of the judges?' Costello asked.

'They must be pretty old,' said Bewley, 'but I haven't looked up their exact ages.'

'I have, though,' said Costello, 'in *Who's Who*. The youngest is seventy-one, the oldest eighty-seven. Their average age is seventy-five.'

'I suppose that explains the fact that after the first half-hour there was never a moment when all five were awake together.'

A book of anecdotes would be incomplete without some mention of the father of the verbal contortion, known as the Irish bull, Sir Boyle Roche.

Roche was not an intellectual. He married a blue-stocking who, it was said, prematurely injured his mental capacity by forcing him to read Gibbon's *Decline and Fall of the Roman Empire*, which puzzled him so much without amusing him, that in his cups he often stigmatised Gibbon as a low fellow who ought to have been kicked out of company wherever he was, for turning people's thoughts away from their prayers and their politics to what the devil himself could make neither head nor tail of.

Although as renowned as Sam Goldwyn for his bulls, there is a school of thought which holds that Roche seldom launched a blunder which did not have an essential truth at its core.

One of his most quoted sayings was pronounced in a debate on the vote of a grant where the opposition claimed that the House had no right to load posterity with a weighty debt for what could in no degree operate to their advantage.

Roche, eager to defend the government asked, 'What, Mr Speaker, and so we are to beggar ourselves for fear of vexing posterity! Now, I would ask the honourable gentleman, and this still more honourable House, why we should put ourselves out of our way to do anything for posterity; for what has posterity done for us?'

The ensuing laughter puzzled him and he hastened to explain that by posterity he did not mean all our ancestors, but those who were to come immediately after them.

Naturally, Boyle Roche supported the Union and declared:

Gentlemen may titther and titther and titther and may think it a bad measure but their heads at present are hot, and will so remain until they grow cool again and so they can't decide right now but when the day of judgement comes, then honourable gentlemen will be satisfied at this most excellent Union. Sir, there is no Levitical degrees between nations and on this occasion I can see neither sin nor shame in marrying our own sister!

Roche was a determined enemy of the French Revolution and took every occasion to denounce it.

'Mr Speaker,' he said once, 'if we once permitted the villainous French masons to meddle with the buttresses and walls of our ancient constitution, they would never stop nor stay, Sir, till they brought the foundation-stones tumbling down about the ears of the nation! If those Gallican villains should invade us, Sir, 'tis on that very table, maybe, these honourable gentlemen might see their own destinies lying in heaps on top of one another! Here perhaps, the murderous marshal-law-men, Marseillois, would break in, cut us to mincemeat, and throw our bleeding heads upon that table, to stare us in the face!'

Sir Boyle was arguing on another occasion for the Habeas Corpus Suspension Bill in Ireland:

It would surely be better, Mr Speaker, to give up not only a part, but, if necessary, even the whole of our constitution to preserve the remainder.

A motion was being debated to expel Lord Edward Fitzgerald sometime in the 1790s for disrespectful expressions regarding the House and the Lord Lieutenant. Fitzgerald apologised but his enemies did not consider it sufficient.

Sir Boyle Roche was racking his brains to find a way out for Lord Edward.

'Mr Speaker,' he said, 'I think the noble young man has no business to make any apology. He is a gentleman, and none such should be asked to make an apology, because no gentleman could mean to give offence.'

Lord Lisle's postillion, Dennis McCarthy, had an action for criminal conversation brought against him by his master. As a result of a very forced construction of the law by the Chief Baron, the jury found damages for £5,000 against him. He did not have such money and was kept in prison for over ten years as a debtor. Strong efforts were made in Parliament to have him released. Sir Boyle, as a last attempt, made a florid speech in his favour, arguing correctly that Lady Lisle, and not Dennis, must have been the real seducer and ending: 'And what, Mr Speaker, was this poor servant's crime? After all, sure, Mr Speaker, it was only doing his master's business by his mistress's orders, and is it not very hard to keep a poor servant in jail for that which if he had not done it, he would have deserved a horse-whipping?'

MAD AND BAD

Professional litigants who appear on their own behalf are universally recognised as pains in the neck to judges, court officials and the legal profession generally. They waste everybody's time because they must be treated with the same courtesy that is extended to 'accidental' litigants, who for some reason or another do not have representation. It is the practice of the bench to lean over backwards to ensure that such cases are not prejudiced by the litigant's lack of knowledge and experience.

Professional litigants generally fall into two categories, the mad and the bad. The mad are just mad. The bad exploit loopholes in the law at the expense of the unwary.

A notorious example of the bad was a Miss Anthony, who flourished towards the end of the last century, who actually made her living by the exploitation of legal technicalities.

Miss Anthony was a woman of extraordinary abilities, insanely directed. At a time when there were no women lawyers, she knew more law than many professionals. She concentrated on the privileges of the common informer, and led a charmed life.

She travelled free on every form of transport, carried away goods from tradesmen, who hastened to assure her that they were gifts, knew of every penalty for technical infringement of the law which put money into the pocket of the busybody who sued, blackmailed the country and lived on assaults, false imprisonments, libels, slanders and similar wrongs.

One fine morning, Miss Anthony arrived at the monastery of Mount Mellary, Co. Waterford to make a retreat which she carried out with exemplary devotion. When the retreat was over, she asked to see the Abbot, explained that she was short of ready cash and wondered if he would loan her £5. She added that she could secure the loan by leaving with the monastery five sheep that she had driven up. Miss Anthony was presentable and well-spoken and the Abbot was a kind man. He lent her the £5 and was too embarrassed to refuse the five sheep. She set off for Dublin promising to send the money as soon as she arrived.

In fact, she returned in person, paid back the £5 and as a token of her esteem and affection she presented him with a document. It was a writ for a £200 penalty payable to the common informer (i.e. Miss Anthony) 'for that he, the Abbot, not being a licenced pawnbroker, had taken in pledge certain chattels, to wit, five sheep'.

On this occasion, her victim could not give in. He consulted a lawyer, who fortunately discovered a minor but sufficient fault which saved the Abbot. For once, the technicalities let Miss Anthony down.

Among the mad and pretty bad were two retired army officers who had both served in India. One had an artificial arm and the other an artificial leg. The former preyed on the high executive officers of the Crown. The other defended them uninstructed. They also litigated *inter se* and, between them, seriously extended the period of the law's delay in Dublin at that time. On one occasion, suit and counter-suit did not satisfy their choleric temperaments and a scuffle broke out in the court-room. Junior Counsel, a nephew of the presiding judge, left the court and bumped into a friend who asked what on earth was going on.

'Oh,' said the young man, 'it's just Williamson with the wooden arm and Harrison with the wooden leg beating one another before my uncle with the wooden head.'

Madmen have their own logic and, sometimes, a basic knowledge of the ordinary rules of procedure is sufficient protection against them. On one occasion, Williamson of the wooden arm applied for a prerogative writ in a matter concerning the Lord Lieutenant.

He appeared before a courteous and diminutive judge from County Down, Mr Justice Andrews, who turned down his application because central to its argument were accusations against the Lord Lieutenant of outrageous behaviour.

The very next day, Mr Williamson was back in court making the same application. Mr Justice Andrews was, as always, the soul of courtesy.

'I am afraid, Mr Williamson,' he said, 'that yesterday I refused to entertain a similar application because I considered that I could not receive an affidavit containing scandalous matter.'

Mr Williamson was not at all put out. In fact, he was sincere and understanding.

'My Lord, I can assure your Lordship that a fresh affidavit has been sworn from which all objectionable matter has been scrupulously eliminated.'

'Very well, Mr Williamson, proceed.'

Mr Williamson made out his case in all seriousness and a plain matter of fact manner.

'The affair, my Lord, is as follows. Yesterday, I made an affidavit before the Right Honorable William Drennan Andrews which was inexplicably refused. I therefore kept a close watch on the said Mr Justice Andrews and last night the reason for his conduct was revealed. At 11.55 p.m., I discovered the said Andrews and the wife of the defendant in this matter misconducting themselves on the steps inside Nelson's Pillar.'

With the exception of the two principals, everybody in the court-room froze. They waited for the explosion. None came.

Applicant and judge looked at one another. One calmly and expectantly, convinced of the merits of his argument.

The other calmly and meditatively. At last, the wee man on the bench spoke kindly and considerately in a tone of firm regret.

'I am afraid, Mr Williamson,' he said, 'you have not been happy in your substitution. It appears that, as an interested party, I am disqualified from hearing this application. You must apply elsewhere.'

———————

There are still people who speak of the good old days, but whether they were good or not depended very much on the position from which one viewed them—which was, all too often, from the dock or the bench. Black humour can sometimes be so black that the humour goes up in smoke.

In the middle of the last century, three men from Kilkenny were accused of stealing malt.

The first man had actually been seen by witnesses wheeling a wheelbarrow with two or three shovelfuls of malt in it. The witnesses were trustworthy, so there was little question of his guilt.

The second man had apparently touched or handled neither the barrow nor the malt. There was not even any evidence offered that he knew that the malt had been stolen. The only evidence offered against him was that he had been seen walking along the road near the man with the wheelbarrow, as had at least twenty other people at the same time. All that could be said against the third man was that at some time, either on the day of the theft or the day after, he had been seen in a public house asking the first accused to buy him a drink.

There should have been no case to answer by the second and third accused, but the judge came from a brewing family and in Kilkenny at that time an accusation of theft of malt was like a hint of witchcraft in New England.

The summing up went like this.

'Against the first,' the judge told the jury, 'the case is clear enough. He was caught with the stolen goods in his possession. In the second case, perhaps, it is not quite so strong, you will think; but it is for you, gentlemen, not for me to judge. You will not forget, gentlemen, he was walking along by the side of the actual thief. It is for you to say what that means.'

If he did not actually wink, he thought a wink.

'Now we come to the third man. Where was he? I must say there is a slight difference between his case and that of the other two men, who might be said to have been caught in the very act, but that's for you, gentlemen, not for me, to decide upon. It is difficult to point out item by item, as it were, the difference between the three cases, very subtle, very subtle, but you will say, gentlemen, whether they were not all mixed up in this robbery—it's for you, gentlemen, not for me.'

The jury convicted instantly.

'I agree with the verdict,' said the judge. 'This is a very bad case, and a town like Kilkenny must be protected against such ruffians as you. No doubt there are degrees of guilt in your several cases, but I do not think that I would be doing my duty to the public if I made any distinction in your sentences. You must all of you undergo a term of five years' penal servitude.'

Counsel for defence could not take it any longer. He leapt to his feet.

'I protest, my Lord, really . . .'

'Yes, really, Mr Callaghan,' said the sadist on the bench.

'But you can't do it, my Lord. You can't give penal servitude for petty larceny. Here is the Act . . .'

And he read it out to the bonehead in the bob-wig.

'. . . unless the prisoner has been guilty of any felony before . . .'

The judge made a face like a child who has been deprived of a toy.

'Oh, very well. You, Gilligan,' he snapped at the actual thief, 'and, you, O'Donoghue, his accessory in the very act, not having been convicted before, I am sorry to say, cannot be sentenced to more than two years' imprisonment with hard labour, and I reduce the sentences in your case to that. But, as to you, O'Farrell,' glaring at the third unfortunate, who was paying dearly for his glass of porter, 'yours is a very bad case, indeed. The jury have found that you were mixed up in this robbery, and I find that you have already been convicted of stealing apples. True, it's a good many years ago, but the leopard doesn't change its spots, and it brings you within the purview of the statute, and therefore your sentence of five years will stand.'

Hardly our cuddly Irish RM.

OUT OF COURT

It is the convention of the Law Library that anyone, even the most senior member, should be prepared to share his knowledge with the most raw junior.

Patrick Lindsay had to write an opinion about a very obscure point concerning tenants for life and the growing of trees. He went for help to a barrister called Charlie Campbell. Unknown to Lindsay, Campbell had a considerable reputation as a fantasist of the Baron Munchausen school.

'I hope you have plenty of time?' asked Campbell and dictated at length various points in connection with the matter. 'Off you go now. You have everything you need there,' he said finally.

Lindsay wrote his opinion but felt that something was not quite right. He asked another barrister, Desmond Bell, who referred him to an Irish case, *Gilmore* v. *The O'Conor Don*.

The judgement was the exact opposite of what Campbell had told him and he noted to his further surprise that Campbell had appeared in the case—as leader on the losing side.

He thought that this might have slipped Campbell's memory and felt that, in fairness, he should remind him of it.

Campbell was not put out.

'The Supreme Court was quite wrong,' he said.

Cecil Lavery was one of the busiest barristers in Ireland. Willie Mason, apart from a few friendly briefs after his call, never set foot in court and spent his days lounging amiably about the Library like Bertie Wooster in the Drones Club chatting to anyone who was willing to spare the time.

Once Lavery returned after an exhausting day in the High Court and immediately proceeded to tunnel into the mountain of briefs that had sprung up in his absence. He felt a presence beside him and, looking up from a complicated Chancery matter, saw Willie standing by expectantly.

'Up to your eyes, I suppose, Cecil?' said Willie.

Lavery put a brave face on it. He put down his pen, pushed his chair back and crossed his legs, 'No, Willie,' he said, 'I have nothing really on hand at the moment.'

'Neither have I, Cecil,' said Willie.

———

Lord Clonmell (later to become as hated as Lord Clare) befriended Jonah Barrington when the latter was still a young barrister.

'Barrington,' he said one day, 'you are married?'

'No doubt,' said Barrington, 'as tight as any person on the face of the earth.'

'All women in the world,' rejoined his Lordship, 'are fond of having their own way.'

'I am firmly of your opinion.'

'Now', contined Lord Clonmell, 'the manner in which all wives are spoiled is by giving them their own way at first; for whatever you accustom them to at the beginning, they will expect ever after. So mind me! I'll tell you the secret of ruling a wife, if known in time. Never do anything for peace sake. If you do, you'll never have another hour's tranquillity but by concessions, mind that.'

'I firmly believe it,' exclaimed Barrington.

'Well, then,' said Clonmell, 'practise it!'

Some time afterward, they met again and Clonmell asked

if the young man had taken his advice.

'No,' said Barrington.

'Why?' inquired his lordship.

'Because,' replied Barrington, 'a philosopher has an easier life than a soldier.'

Subsequently, Lord Clonmell married a second wife, a Miss Lawless, and apparently no husband in Ireland adhered less to his own theories than did Lord Clonmell.

Once, at the bar-mess on circuit, a barrister called Daly was speaking rather indecorously of Mr William Johnson in his absence. Daly was tartly and very properly asked by Mr Justice Jebb, 'Why do you say such things of Mr Johnson behind his back?'

'Because,' replied Mr Daly, 'I would not hurt his feelings by saying them to his face.'

A barrister on the north-eastern circuit many years ago was distinguished for a combination of pretentiousness and preciousness which drove his earthier brothers to distraction. While they were happy to talk about football or horse racing, he insisted on bringing artistic topics to the mess table. He claimed to be particularly fond of music and was inevitably disappointed with the impromptu concerts which took place after bar dinners.

One evening, having sat through 'Abdul the Bul-Bul Ameer' and 'The Ball of Killiemuir', he inquired plaintively: 'Does anyone know "The Last Rose of Summer"? It affects me so much whenever I hear it, it quite carries me away.'

'Will someone, for God's sake, hum it,' cried a flushed colleague.

When barristers are not in court or the Law Library, they are not infrequently to be found at racecourses, in city centre hotels and restaurants and, in the old days, at the theatre, opera and music-hall.

There are many stories of visits to the theatre after bar dinners where the automatic reflex of pungent comment could not be repressed.

One such occurred during a performance of *Rigoletto* in Cork Opera House. The tenor had also been out to dinner before the performance and could be described as feeling no pain. During the first act, he was seen to stumble and grab at scenery and divas where the libretto did not call for it. Waving his arms, he almost beheaded the baritone at one point and was obviously asleep in the second act. Before the curtain rose for the third act, the theatre manager appeared and apologised to the audience that Signor Farfalli was unable to continue since he had been stricken by a sudden attack of malaria. A junior counsel, in whom the glow of the evening's claret was beginning to dull, remarked *sotto voce*:

'God, I wish I had a bottle of that.'

On another occasion, another tenor, who had passed his prime, knew he would not make the top note, so he started to wave his hands about in an attempt to distract the audience from his performance.

A music-loving judge in the front row slapped his knee with his programme and snapped as he might in court, 'Don't point at it, man. Sing it!'

Opera was not always available and, in towns like Ballyshannon or Athy, the only diversion for tired and emotional barristers was the fit-up play performing *Murder in the Red Barn* or *Arrah-na-Pogue*.

No matter how much they had drunk, the gentlemen of the bar never shook off their particular law-bound world view.

Early in the century, a group of barristers, bored with briefs, whist and each other, trooped off late to a performance of a standard melodrama: brave but stupid hero, virtuous heroine and intelligent but despicable moustachioed villain. The members of the circuit arrived in the hall just as as Sir Roderick was waving a deed under the terrified heroine's nose and announcing that he controlled her home and lands and unless she . . .

At which point, the heroine clasped her bosom, rolled her eyes and carolled, 'What shall I do–oo? What shall I doo–oo?'

Quick as a flash, one of the barristers called out, 'Object that the document is insufficiently stamped.'

A Visit.

Archibald Hamilton Rowan was a gentleman of most respectable family and of ample fortune. He was also a man given to espousing causes. One such was a very young girl called Mary Neil, who had been ill-treated by a person unknown, aided by a woman. One Lord Carhampton was supposed to be the transgessor, but there was no proof of this.

The quixotic Hamilton Rowan took up the cause of Mary Neil with a zeal and an enthusiastic perseverance worthy of the mad knight of La Mancha. Day and night the ill-treatment of this girl was the subject of his thoughts, his actions, his dreams. He went about preaching a crusade in her favour and eventually obtained a conviction of the woman as accessory to the crime. She was executed.

Mary Neil, however, remained unprovided for and there were still people who did not believe her and claimed that she was an imposter. This hurt the feelings, philanthropy and pride of Hamilton Rowan and he vowed personal vengeance against all her calumniators, high and low.

At this time, about twenty young barristers, including Jonah Barrington, had formed a dinner club in Dublin where they got drunk regularly on claret smuggled in from the Isle of Man. One day the servant informed them that a gentleman below stairs desired to be admitted for a moment. They assumed that it was another barrister who wanted to join their party and asked that he be shown up.

To their great surprise this was not the case. Instead, a man who might have served as a model of Hercules appeared, his gigantic limbs conveying the idea of almost supernatural strength, his shoulders, arms and broad chest the very emblems of muscular energy, his flat, rough countenance, overshadowed by dark eyebrows, completing one of the finest and most formidable figures they had ever seen. He was very well dressed; close by his side stalked a shaggy Newfoundland dog of corresponding magnitude, with hair a foot long, and who, if he was hungry, seemed well able to devour a barrister or two without overcharging his stomach. As he entered, indeed, he alternately looked at the barristers and then up at his master, as only awaiting orders to have a go. His master held in his hand a large, yellow, knotted club, slung by a leathern thong around his great wrist; he also had a small-sword by his side.

The man walked deliberately up to the table and bowed politely. There was a short pause, during which he looked around in a manner which, if not exactly stern, was not one calculated to set their minds at ease as to his or his dog's intentions.

'Gentlemen,' he said at length in a tone and with an air that was so mild and courteous, so polished even, that it seemed to give the lie to his threatening figure. 'Gentlemen, I have heard with very great regret that some members of this club have been so indiscreet as to calumniate the character of Mary Neil, which, from the part that I have taken, I feel identified with my own. If any present has done so, I doubt not he will have the candour and the courage to avow it. Who avows it?'

The dog looked up at him again expectantly. Rowan returned the glance but contented himself for the present with patting the animal's head and remained silent. So were the young barristers. There was no question of consulting as to what reply to make. A few of the company whispered to their neighbours and one or two stole a fruit-knife under the tablecloth but no one replied. There were eighteen of them and, since no one would or could answer for the others, it would have taken eighteen replies to satisfy the giant's single query. It was possible that some there could not have replied to Rowan's satisfaction and still stuck to the truth. He repeated his demand three times, raising his tone higher each time, 'Does any gentleman avow it?'

A faint buzz circulated round the room, but there was no answer. For once, these barristers were at a loss for words.

At length, Rowan said in a loud voice that he must suppose that if any gentleman had made observations or assertions against Mary Neil's character, he would have had the courage and spirit to avow it; therefore he would take it for granted that his information was erroneous and, in that point of view, he regretted having alarmed their society.

Without another word, he bowed low three times, and retired backwards towards the door, his dog also backing out with equal politeness, where with a final salaam he ended the interview.

On the first of his departing bows, the diners scrambled to their feet and bent over in absolute silence till they almost touched the table with their noses. They kept this up until he was out of the room. Three or four of the company then ran to the window to make sure that Rowan and the dog were clear off into the street, and no sooner were they sure of this, than there was a general roar of laughter and a burst of conversation.

They discussed the visit for the rest of the night, the most important question being, who had behaved the politest on the occasion?

'But not one word was said,' Barrington remarks, 'as to who had behaved the stoutest.'

Four friends went into business together; one had the money and the others had the experience. After some time, they had the money and he had the experience. He then suffered a heart attack and died.

The three survivors got together and admitted that they

had been too clever. The unspoken admission was that perhaps it was their sharp practice that had caused their friend's death.

'We must make it up to him,' said one.

'We should pay him back,' said the second.

'He's dead. He has no family. It would be different if he had left a wife and kids,' said the third, a solicitor. 'The money would only go to some distant cousin in America.'

'No, I think that we should be punished.'

'But how?' asked the solicitor.

'I know,' said the first man, 'when we bury him, let's bury the feckin' money we made out of him.'

Everybody agreed that this was be the proper thing to do.

The day of the funeral came and after the priest and the mourners had gone away, the three friends stayed behind.

'Here's my percentage,' said the first friend and scattered the notes over the coffin.

'Here's mine,' said the second and did the same.

'And mine,' said the solicitor and wrote and signed a cheque which he dropped into the grave.

When Patrick Lindsay, later to be TD, first Minister for the Gaeltacht and Master of the High Court, set out from his lodgings on his first day at University College, Galway, he asked a passer-by where he would find the university and was told that it was a big building across the bridge. He crossed the bridge and knocked at the gate of the first impressive building he met. A little slide opened in the gate and a cross voice asked him what he wanted. Lindsay wanted to know if he had come to the University and if he could be admitted.

'No,' said the man inside, 'this is the County Jail— you're not ready for this place yet.'

PUNS

Far from being the lowest form of wit, the pun, at one time, seemed to be the only form recognised in society. Legal anecdotes are as studded with puns as a barmbrack with raisins.

The Duke of Wellington has at least one pun attributed to him.

He had an accident and lost an eye which he kept in spirits of wine to preserve it. One day he met a friend who asked him how he was.

'Oh, Lord Cairns asked me the same question yesterday,' the Duke replied, 'and I said "I am rather depressed but I believe my eye is in pretty good spirits."'

John Philpot Curran was arguing a case and behind him in the court was a very tall and very skinny colleague who had originally intended to take holy orders but had switched to the law. The judge interrupted Curran and pointed out that the point at issue touched on ecclesiastical law and he would need some authorites on it.

Curran instantly replied, 'I can refer your Lordship to a high authority behind me who was once intended for the Church, though in my opinion he was better fitted for the steeple.'

Curran was once examining Lundy Foot, a celebrated Dublin tobacconist whose main claim to fame was as inventor or compounder of Foot's snuff which bore his name.

Curran asked the snuff-merchant a difficult question. Lundy Foot hesitated and Curran pounced.

'Lundy,' he said, 'isn't that a poser? A deuce of a *pinch*, Lundy, wouldn't you say?'

Poor unfortunate Lord Kilwarden had no aptitude whatsoever for punning, but continued to excruciate his friends with his hopeless attempts at word play. The best he ever managed was to call Curran 'Gooseberry'!

If the United States of America and Britain are two countries divided by a common language, this is even more true of Britain and Ireland. One could almost pity the poor Englishman who comes to Ireland full of good intentions and finds himself lost at sea without a life-belt.

This was the case with Lord Redesdale, ancestor of Nancy Mitford. He came to Ireland as Lord Chancellor and gave a dinner for the judges and King's Counsel. Having heard that the members of the Irish bar were considered to be extremely witty (they still think so), and wanting if possible to adapt himself to their habits, his Lordship gathered together some of his best bar-remarks to repeat to the company as occasion might offer. He knew himself that he was incapable of humour, but was determined at least to be entertaining.

He began by telling them all after dinner that he had been a Welsh judge and had found great difficulty in pronouncing the double consonants which occur in Welsh proper names.

'After much trial,' he said, 'I found that the difficulty was mastered by moving the tongue alternately from one dog-tooth to the other.'

This fell flat as a spade and when Toler (whom we have met before) tried to be clever in response, his attempt fell even flatter.

Lord Redesdale's next remark was that when he was a lad, cock-fighting was the fashion, and that both ladies and gentlemen went full dressed to the cock-pits, the ladies being in hoops.

'I see now, my lord,' said Toler, 'it was then that the term "cock-a-hoop" was invented.'

A general laugh burst forth, which rather discomposed the learned Chancellor. He sat silent for a while, until skating became the subject of conversation, when he rallied and with an air of triumph said that in his boyhood all danger was avoided, for before they began to skate they alway put blown bladders under their arms, and so, if the ice happened to break, they were buoyant and saved.

'Ay, my lord,' Toler came in again, 'that's what we call "blather-am-skate" in Ireland.'

The conversation continued but, although he remained extremely courteous, there was a distinct impression that the Lord Chancellor wished the Irish lawyers in their respective homes.

———————

Life at the bar and racing have always been closely associated, perhaps because every trial is in a sense a gamble, and waiting for a jury to reach a verdict is as thrilling and nerve-racking as any steeplechase. A Queen's Counsel, who also farmed in Queen's County, not only kept a stable of fine horses but was also an inveterate punster. He liked nothing better than to walk guests around his land and to tantalise them with the names of his animals. He had a mare called Saltfish because, as he explained, she was such a capital mare for a fast day. Another was called Naples. She was a beautiful bay. Yet another was Morning Star since, as he informed his by now sagging guests, she was a roarer!

———————

One day another imported judge, who took a boyish glee in punning, met a friend, Mr Maylem, while they were both on holiday in Bray.

He asked Maylem if he had been bathing and the latter explained that his doctor had ordered him not to bathe.

'Oh then,' said Erskine, 'you are *malum prohibitum*' (an expressly forbidden wrong).

'But my wife,' continued the unfortunate Maylem, no doubt to calm this madman, 'does bathe.'

'That means,' said the judge, 'that she was *malum in se*' (an intrinsic wrong).

RELIGION

Judge Warren took a poisonous pleasure in savaging young barristers. He would fire scathing remarks at a little rabbit struggling with stage-fright, regardless of what might result. A. M. Sullivan, on his first appearance before Warren, had years of political platform and press behind him, did not regard himself as a rabbit and probably conveyed that fact to Warren. He was duly attacked.

Some question arose about an interlineation in a will by which a legacy was increased if the donee obtained a Fellowship. Warren observed that it was clear that Sullivan's education had not enabled him to understand the qualification of a Fellow. Sullivan replied that his sole source of knowledge on the point was derived from papal definition. As this supposed allusion to the Pope, whose name he hated, the judge hissed, 'I am not aware that His Holiness defines academic distinction.'

'Not *the* Pope, but Pope:
"Worth makes the man, and want of it the fellow;
The rest is all but leather or prunella."'

Sullivan continued with his argument, delighted to observe that Warren was cudgelling his brain for the retort that the remark demanded, but obviously unable to find one.

Leslie Foster was appointed a Commissioner for Education in the 1840s with an enormous salary. Taken together with his vast emoluments as Counsel for the

Commissioners of Customs and Excise, his income would have made earnings at trivialities such as the twentieth-century Beef Tribunal pale into insignificance.

His ostensible remit was to report on the state of Roman Catholic schools and the progress of education but, since he was known to be a bigot, this was not the most fortunate appointment. Foster's private object was to bring out whatever was unfavourable to the Irish priesthood.

He met his match when he came up against the Rev. Mr Kenny, the Superior of the Jesuits in Ireland, who was summoned to appear before the Commissioners for Education. Although Kenny's outward appearance did not conform to the stereotypical picture of the handsome aristocratic son of Loyola, he had been educated in Palermo and had a Sicilian suavity of manner which the Prince of Lampedusa would have recognised. With a blend of affected humility and cutting sarcasm, he countered all Foster's questions, apparently blunting the edge of his sarcasm by his soft voice and his prayerful manner of holding his clasped hands up to his chin, while he regretted much more in sorrow than in anger the lamentable ignorance and delusion of someone who could, in the nineteenth century, trot out such preposterous and out-dated notions.

Because Foster had been downright offensive in some of his questions, one of the Commissioners felt it his duty to apologise on behalf of the others.

'I regret', he said, 'that the imperious sense of duty of our brother Commissioner induced him to commit an apparent violation of the canons of good breeding.'

'Holy Ignatius', said Kenny, crossing his arms meekly on his breast, 'I am not offended—I never saw a more simple-minded gentleman in my life.'

There was a time in the first half of the nineteenth century when the call of more than the odd Catholic to the bar was a matter of excitement and curiosity, and when in the same day two types of oath might be sworn by aspirants for admission to the bar. One would protest before the Chief Justice and heaven against the damnable idolatry of the Church of Rome; the other would limit itself to expressions of loyalty to the Crown. It was a time when the Chief Justice, if he heard the watered-down oath more than once, had a look of distaste if not of fear on his face, and the faintest of welcoming smiles for the newly called advocate was achieved only by an intense effort of will.

It was said that on a day when four Catholics were admitted one after the other, Mr Serjeant Lefroy, alarmed at the repeated omissions of the pious denunciations of the Virgin Mary, by which the laws and liberties of Ireland were sustained, actually paused in the very act of putting a fee into his pocket and lifted his eyes up to heaven in silent prayer or imprecation.

Mr William Bellew was a devout and unostentatious but rigorously practising Catholic in those sectarian days. He was so low-key about his religious duties that they attracted no notice. He was never one of those lost sheep whose return to the flock give joy in heaven. If another barrister went to communion, the news flashed around Dublin immediately and at all the Catholic parties the ladies would describe in minute detail the collected aspect, the combined expression of penitence and humility, the clasped hands and the uplifted eyes of the counsel. When Mr Bellew attended the sacraments no one bothered to comment.

There was only one occasion when, inadvertently, he flaunted his beliefs. One Ash Wednesday, the court was kept waiting for Mr Bellew, and the Master of the Rolls began to grow impatient. Finally, the old barrister rushed into court in such a hurry that he forgot to wipe off his ashes.

Bellew's face was cadaverous and skull-like, full of what contemporaries called 'melancholy reminiscences' but when the Master of the Rolls raised his eyes from a notice which he had been reading and looked Bellew straight in the face, his mouth dropped open.

Everybody saw the judge start, turned to stare at Bellew and saw traced in broad sepulchral lines, in ebony ash, in the very centre of his forehead, surmounted by an ample and fully powdered wig, the black and, to them, appalling emblem of the cross. The burning cross upon the forehead of the sorcerer in *The Monk* could not have produced a more terrifying effect.

The six clerks stood astonished. The registrar was petrified and, while Mr Driscoll explained the matter to Mr Serjeant Lefroy, Sir William McMahon, with some abruptness of tone, declared that he would not go beyond the motion.

———

Throughout the nineteenth century, to an extent that is inconceivable today, religious beliefs and blatant sectarianism influenced politics and legal careers. A prominent barrister of the time was one Edward Morphy, who never attempted to conceal his contempt for Roman Catholics. The trial judge was William O'Brien who, in contrast, was a militant RC.

Morphy was having some difficulty with a witness who obviously did not know his station and answered questions as if he were chatting with counsel in a public house.

'Sure and I did, Mr Murphy. Not at all, Mr Murphy, I never seen the man at all.'

More and more, Morphy was showing his irritation, not only with the familiarity of the witness, but also with the perversion of his name. O'Brien, who was enjoying every minute of Morphy's discomfiture, allowed the dialogue to continue as long as he decently could before gently rebuking the witness.

'You must not call this gentleman "Mr Murphy",' he informed the witness. 'His name is "Morphy". That is the Protestant for "Murphy".'

Tim Healy, who found himself on the side of the Bishops during the Parnellite split, once remarked: 'The Irish bishops are individually virtuous and sapient men, wise in precept and impeccable in practice. But 'tis a great misfortune that they should always fix their meetings for an occasion when the Holy Ghost happens to be engaged elsewhere.'

Frank Shields was an elegant barrister with the manners and habits of an age fifty years before his birth. He had had an expensive education with the Jesuits and did not at all sound like a lad from Loughrea.

Once he was appointed commissioner to take evidence from a witness who was too ill to attend court.

The commission was held in a village of thatched cottages called Glengowla, about five miles on the Clifden side of Oughterard.

Patrick Lindsay was attempting to set aside a deed made by a father in favour of his son while his wife was out of the house. When the wife discovered the existence of the deed, she immediately consulted a solicitor who briefed Lindsay.

The father was tucked up in the tiny bedroom off the kitchen.

Frank Shields produced his commissioner's equipment. No biro or tape recorder for him on such occasions. Any evidence that he collected was recorded on thick notepaper by means of a square bottle of bright blue Stephens ink and a Pickwick or Owl or Waverly pen. He looked around for a table on which to carry out his task but table there was none. The closest substitute was an old trunk which had obviously been brought back from Boston or Springfield, Mass. It was serrated and lumpy on top. With difficulty he found a flat square two inches on which to balance his bottle and laid the steel-nibbed pen beside it. A board had to be found to support his notepaper.

Once the commissioner had finished his elaborate preparations, Lindsay began to examine the old man beginning with his name, address and age. The answer to the final question was, 'I'll be eighty-six coming MacDara's Day.'

Lindsay could not hear the scrape of Frank's pen. He looked over at him and found Frank to be completely nonplussed.

'I beg your pardon, Pat. Did he say Derby Day?'

'Hah,' said Lindsay. 'The poor oul' natives mustn't rank high in Jesuit hagiology.'

SEX

Before the Land Acts effectively wiped out the landlords, there were good land agents and many very bad ones. In Munster there was one who used his power over his tenantry to further his own special interests. If a tenant had a pretty daughter, he was given the alternative of eviction or letting his daughter go into service in the agent's house. If the broken man sent his daughter, the sequence of service was kitchen, table, bed.

The agent kept a record of his victims and paid the Board of Guardians for the keep of his illegitimate children. He was brought to court only once and on the witness table in the public court he calmly produced his book, ran his finger down the list of conquests and stated that it contained no record of the girl in question.

Unlike many, this agent died in his bed.

Similar abuse was attributed to Lord Leitrim who was, in fact, murdered but over land not lechery.

Two English tourists driving through the country in the last century were pointed out the spot where the old lecher had been assassinated. They began to deplore the depravity and savagery of the murder, but the driver of their car cut them short.

'There wasn't a young one round here that was safe from him. As soon as they were old enough for it, he had their shifts over their heads.' And he gave them chapter and verse for half an hour.

The Englishmen were amazed and horrified in true British fashion and one asked, 'If any fraction of these stories is true, why was the ruffian not shot long ago?'

'Well, your honour', said the jarvey, 'what was everybody's business was nobody's business.'

Kanturk litigants were obsessed with the need for corroboration of their evidence. A bizarre example arose in an action for 'criminal conversation', i.e. where a husband looked for monetary compensation from another man for alienating his wife's affections.

A middle-aged farmer, who was married to a very young wife, started off one evening to go to a distant fair. For some reason, he came back after dark and, looking through the shutters, saw a young man, a rate collector, having supper with the young wife, who happened to be sitting on his knee. The farmer had two choices: to rush in before banter turned to bonking, or find witnesses and have a cause of action and a substantial award in his favour.

Mammon triumphed over Eros and, being a Kanturk man, he went to look for corroborative witnesses. He felt that the RIC, the Royal Irish Constabulary, would be the surest and safest and, even though the nearest barracks was several hours away, he turned his trap around and set off.

When they got back, the young man was still there and the policemen could testify to as much.

However, when the case came to court, it turned out that there had been no previous assignation. The rate collector and the wife had not known each other before and it was only an accident to his horse that had brought him to the house. Whether or not anything happened which might have alienated the wife's affections from her husband, the judge was so outraged at the husband's scale of priorities that he persuaded the jury to find against him.

The verdict was afterwards set aside, but it set in train a family feud that lasted for many years.

A traveller was charged with a sexual offence against a young girl after a horse fair. He protested his innocence indignantly and denied that he could ever have 'interfered' with young Molly Joyce.

Molly had been a good witness, however, and counsel had enough material to conduct a searching cross-examination with the result that the indignation was narrowed down to contempt for the accusation that Connors had done 'de boul' t'ing' with her.

'So you say,' pressed counsel, 'but you know that this young girl told the truth in court today. It's time for you to tell the truth too. What did you do to her then?'

The traveller pondered on the effect a small admission might have and then conceded, 'Well, yer Honour, maybe I did give her a flick of the boss.'

This caught the judge's fancy and, when the man had been duly convicted, he said to him,

'Tim Connors, I'm sentencing you for the offence of which you have been found guilty. Three months for yourself and three months for the boss. Six months in all.'

Specialisation exists in the legal world as much as in the medical, and just as one would not ask a pediatrician to perform a heart transplant, so practitioners in the fields of contract law, criminal law and chancery stray into each others' worlds at their peril. Unfortunately this has not always been remembered when sending judges out to cope with the world beyond the Four Courts.

The result of sending the wrong judge to do the wrong job was shown many years ago when one Judge Boyd went on assize to Ennis with little knowledge and less practical experience of criminal law or of rural Ireland.

Among the civil bill appeals listed was one where the plaintiff had brought an action for seduction against the defendant. In those days such an action had to be approached in a technical and artificial form. The woman, through her father, accused the man of being the father of her child. The County Court judge had taken the measure of the complainant and her father and had sent them packing.

The woman appealed and the appeal came before Boyd. Sobbing and sighing, she recounted how she had been wronged, but admitted afterwards to the young man's counsel that she might have been wronged on a regular basis by many another.

The terrified respondent, who came from decent people, denied everything and, with one exception, it was pretty obvious to everyone in court who was telling the truth. Unfortunately, the one exception was Boyd. These were the days when virginity was endemic among country folk until late middle age, a fact unknown to the urban judge.

'You say you never had anything to do with this girl?'

'Never, my Lord.'

'How old are you?'

'I'm twenty-six, my Lord.'

'Have you ever had anything to do with any other girl?'

'Never, my Lord.'

'Oh, my goodness! Twenty-six and you never had anything to do with a girl! Do you expect me to believe that? Or anything else you say? I'll reverse this dismiss, and give a decree for £50 and costs!'

His satisfaction at his own astuteness was even greater than the pleasure of punishing a hypocrite.

———————

There are no stories in this book about women barristers for the reason that until the twentieth century they did not exist. The legal world was an exclusively male world and, even in the 1930s, a woman who had been competently carrying out her father's duties as Clerk of the Court was denied the post on his death purely on the grounds of her sex.

Great care was taken during Queen Victoria's reign and for some considerable time afterwards to preserve 'ladies' from the seamier side of life. Kevin O'Higgins, when Minister for Justice and External Affairs in the 1920s, barred women from juries for their own protection.

One excuse for keeping women out of court, particularly during criminal trials, was the manner in which habitual criminals defended themselves. Their main defence was seldom on the facts but in relation to character, to show that they were purer than the driven snow and that their accusers were blackguards. The only moral deficiency that would seriously impair the credibility of a witness was a record of offence against the virtue of chastity. Suggestions of sexual transgression were always made in sound Anglo-Saxon terminology and with a wealth of obscene detail.

At the Winter Assizes in Cork in 1893, the judge, William O'Brien, sent for Richard Adams, who was prosecuting and asked him to put on some particularly innocuous case next morning because he intended to bring two young ladies in to sit on the bench with him.

Adams gave an undertaking that nothing unseemly would happen.

A prisoner was indicted for the theft of a pair of boots from a common lodging house. The owner of the boots was examined in chief and all seemed well until the witness commenced to volunteer some statements of an improper character relating to the prisoner, i.e that he was nothing but 'a little bum-boy'.

The prisoner retaliated with a detailed account of the sexual rapaciousness of the witness, his exploitation of the other young men in the lodging house and his own refusal to respond to the very obscene invitation extended to him which resulted in this malicious charge.

Judge O'Brien jumped out of his chair with a scream.

'Begone, girls,' he exclaimed and he hustled the girls, who were beginning to get the gist of things, off the bench.

He then returned to his seat, glared at the Crown Prosecutor and repeated three times, 'Adams, you ruffian!'

Adams looked perfectly innocent, but his reputation as a practical joker deprived him of the benefit of the doubt.

On another occasion in Cork an action was due to come up before Peter O'Brien which had attracted the attention of Cork society. The gallery was full of attentive young ladies. Unfortunately there was one more criminal case to go. The Crown Prosecutor, as was his habit, whistled a few bars of an operatic aria and looked hesitant.

'I don't feel very happy in putting forward my next case in this assembly,' he told the judge and twirled his pince-nez at the end of its chain.

'Then adjourn it,' said Peter.

'Can't. It's a custody case without bail.'

'Then go on with it. What is the charge?'

'Larceny.'

'Go on with it.'

Two unsavoury-looking men and a young woman appeared in the dock. The jury was sworn.

Captain Jones of the schooner *Betsy* then testified that he had come ashore on 13 May wearing a large gold watch and chain, that they had been attached to his waistcoat when he went to sleep that night but when he woke up next morning they were gone.

'Very good,' said the judge, 'you may go down.'

The Clerk of the Crown and Peace, Henry T. Wright, stood up, screwed his monocle in his eye and announced: 'The prisoners have a constitutional right to cross-examine.'

'They have,' said Peter. 'Do any of you prisoners want to ask any questions? The witness so far has proved nothing against you.'

One of the men indicated that he had questions and proceeded to question Captain Jones about his meeting with them and their girlfriends on the night of the 13th, about the drinks that they had together and the suggestions that the Captain made to the girl in the dock and her responses. Everybody was embarrassed except Captain Jones.

The judge interrupted.

'It is clear,' he said, 'that this is going to be a very unpleasant case for ladies to listen to, so we shall stop it to let any who wish to retire to do so.'

None went. There were hundreds outside waiting to get in for the fashionable action.

'Very well,' said Peter. 'They like it. Go ahead.'

This encouraged the prisoner. He developed his theme, asking the Captain to tell how they went to a shebeen and the sort of conversation and foreplay that took place there, culminating in the female prisoner and the captain going off into the night together. The Captain appeared to be the only unconcerned person in the court. He answered the questions with extreme candour. He was evidently quite amused at this investigation, quite unconscious that it had anything to do with the truth of his story. He accepted the proceedings as presumably regular in the country in which he found himself.

The interrogator started to speculate on what took place when the Captain and the girl got back to his lodgings, but the judge could stand no more.

'No decent woman should stay here,' he said. 'Get out.'

And they got out.

SOLICITORS

Already in the days of Charles I, this much maligned branch of the profession was alleged 'to have arisen in great part out of the suits in the dread Star Chamber', to have been 'of doubtful legality and [its] character not over good'.

A barrister (naturally) claimed that:

> In our age there are stepped up a new sort of people called solicitors unknown to the records of the law who like the grasshoppers of Egypt devour the whole land and are express maintainers and cannot justify their maintenance upon any action brought; I mean not where a lord or gentleman employed his servant to solicit his cause, for he could justify the doing thereof; but I mean those which are common solicitors of causes, and set up a new profession, not being allowed in any court, or, at least, not in this court where they seek causes; and these are not retainers of causes but devourers of men's estates by contention and prolonging suits to make them without end.

Frank Fitzgibbon was an expert on income tax law. He was once asked for an opinion by a solicitor in County Cavan whom he had reason to dislike. Some time later he wrote back and said that the opinion was ready and would be sent on receipt of his fee of one hundred guineas.

The opinion, when it arrived, consisted of one sentence.

'This company should appeal the assessment, it will certainly succeed.'

The solicitor wrote back angrily demanding a longer opinion, Fitzpatrick's reasoning and a list of authorities.

Frank wrote back, 'My reasoning is my own and can wait until we are in court.'

When asked why he had written in this way, he replied, 'Once that damn fellow had the opinion, he would send it round to all his accomplices in Cavan and they would all get free advice at my expense.'

A solicitor had a case in Galway involving an English insurance company. An insurance man had come over from London to make sure that nothing went wrong. He was staying at the Railway Hotel in Eyre Square about half a mile from the courthouse. It was a lovely fresh morning and, when the solicitor came to meet him at the hotel, they decided to walk to the court. They had come as far as an imposing classical building when the solicitor excused himself for a moment and disappeared inside. Three minutes later he was out again.

'Shall we not go in now? This is the courthouse, isn't it?' asked the insurance man.

'No, this isn't the courthouse. This is the Franciscan Friary.'

'Franciscan Friary? What on earth were you doing in there?'

'I just nipped in and said a quick little prayereen for the success of the Phoenix Insurance Company.'

'Well, I certainly hope you got through to head office more quickly than I can.'

Managing clerks were a power in the land and knew more about the practicalities of the law than many young solicitors with strings of letters after their name. They could cut through legal problems in ways that were not to be found in any calf-bound volume or black letter learning.

One such was Paddy Fanning, a managing clerk in Naas. He once asked the young Patrick MacKenzie to advise on a case concerning the payment of Social Welfare stamps. MacKenzie wrote an opinion stating that the client, a rich English thoroughbred breeder, was not obliged to pay. Subsequently, he discovered that he had overlooked a recent Act which, in fact, made the client liable. He went straight to Fanning and admitted his mistake as if he were announcing the end of the world.

'Have you ever made a mistake like this before?' asked Fanning. 'Not checked all your Acts?'

MacKenzie said truthfully that he had never made such a mistake before and would never make it again.

Fanning picked up the receiver of the old-fashioned telephone on his desk.

'Hello, is that you, Mr P? Very well thank you and yourself? You remember that little matter that you have pending in the Circuit Court. That's the very one, yes. You know there's very little in it in the heel of the hunt. It occurred to me that it could look bad if you were seen to be going to such lengths over a trifle. It could carry the wrong message, if you take my meaning. If you'll excuse me saying so, trust and credit are very important in this area and in your line of business.'

There was a pause.

'I quite agree. I didn't want to suggest it myself but I think you've taken the right decision.'

He then rang the opposing solicitor, settled the case and, when he had put down the phone, nodded to MacKenzie. 'Anything else I can do for you?'

Patrick MacKenzie, on his first day on circuit in Wicklow, lunched with the State Solicitor, Gus Cullen, who had been prosecuting some young fellows for creating a disturbance in a public place. He had called for the full rigour of the law in respect of all but one of them.

'They're all blackguards, m'Lord,' he said, 'except young Behan there. Normally now, he's a quiet young lad and comes from good stock. I'd say now it was the bad influence of the others got him into this scrape.'

At lunch, the other solicitors were teasing him for this favouritism and wanted to know why he had singled out this young man.

'Arrah,' said Cullen simply, 'sure his father is a client of mine with a fine farm of land and I have his will in my safe.'

Conflict of interest, thy name is legion.

A crafty barrister once said on his retirement, 'I have never failed to conduct a case in accordance with the directions of the managing clerk. I have lost a great many cases, but I have never lost a solicitor.'

A man went to see a solicitor with a legal problem concerning an inheritance. Unfortunately, the solicitor whom he consulted was already involved in the matter on another side and could not represent him. He was extremely helpful, however, and offered to write a note to the other lawyer in the town. He wrote it, sealed it in an envelope and the young man set off across the town. On the way, his curiosity got the better of him. Would the note give him some indication of his chances in the affair? He had to see what what inside. He opened it and read,

'Dear Ciarán,
Here is a plump pigeon for the plucking. Make the best of it.
Kind regards,
Iosagán.'

The famous Judge Comyn was hearing an appeal from the District Court. A District Justice had ordered a young girl to be imprisoned for the theft of her employers' jewellery and some silver spoons. The defending solicitor explained that she had fallen in love with a man who had promised to marry her and that it was he who had persuaded her to carry out the theft. The jewellery had been recovered but the false-hearted friend had disappeared with the spoons and the girl could not, or more likely would not, say where he was. The solicitor painted such a picture of deception and betrayal, of innocence being abused and misplaced loyalty, that there was scarcely a dry eye in the court.

'Very touching, Mr Louth, very moving,' said the judge, 'the girl was hard done by. But she'll have to play her part. She'll have to produce those spoons. Lovely things, you'll not see the like of them nowadays.'

'I understand, m'Lord, and I'm sure my client understands too. May I have five minutes with the girl?'

Permission was granted and in dumb play the solicitor and his client could be seen arguing, he waving his hands and his papers in exasperation, she shaking her head stubbornly.

'Her answer, Mr Louth?' said the judge when the solicitor had returned.

'Ah, this is not the first time, I've spoken to her, m'Lord. I'll tell you what, no man could have pressed her more, I've pressed her and I've pressed her and I've pressed her upside down and inside out and I can't get a spoon out of her.'

The spoonless girl was bound over to be of good behaviour.

———————

In the early days of motoring, there was substantial prejudice against motorists and anything, however irrelevant, went in cross-examination. The driver was fair game.

A farmer returning from a fair with a few pints in him, half-asleep in the cart that the old mare was pulling home at her leisure, was injured in a collision with a motor-car owned by a well-known Dublin physician. The accident happened at a sharp turn in a country road many miles from the city, at a late hour on a winter's night.

'Come sorr', commenced the small but resonant leader for the plaintiff, 'are you the great Doctor L—?'

'My name is L— and I am a doctor.'

'Answer my question. Are you the great Doctor L—?'

'I do not so call myself.'

'Ah, sorr, don't trifle with me. Don't you consider yourself the great Doctor L—?'

The judge stepped in to put him back on the track.

'Very well, I bow to his Lordship's suggestion. Whether you are the great Doctor L— or the small Doctor L—, what were you doing on the Ashford Road at that hour of the night?'

'I was driving out to visit a patient.'

'Come, sorr, do you swear that?'

'Of course I do.'

'It is not "of course", sorr. What is the name of the patient?'

'My Lord, must I name the patient?'

His Lordship told him that this was not necessary.

'Very well, never mind his name, but he was a patient?'

'He was.'

'What was he suffering from?'

'Really . . .'

'Ah, come, sorr. If you had a patient, you must know what he was suffering from. Was it smallpox?'

'No, sir, it was not.'

Counsel turned to the bench.

'In charity to the patient, I will asume that it was only the *chicken* pox.'

The cross-examination continued, with dark hints of the infamous crimes that alone could account for the presence of an eminent medical man on the Ashford Road at half-past ten at night. The jury was impressed and awarded damages accordingly.

Legal battlefields are littered with the corpses of those whose strokes fail to come off.

Once in Cork a solicitor was engaged in an action against the local gas company for flooding his client's premises with sulphurated hydrogen. The solicitor felt, no doubt quite rightly, that no one who had not smelled the stuff could understand what his client had suffered. Accordingly, without saying anything to his counsel, getting the permission of the judge or entering the object as an exhibit, he handed a friendly juror a glass retort containing sulphurated hydrogen at some pressure.

Unfortunately, in the jury room the retort fell and smashed to pieces. The fumes filled the room and the twelve jurors were almost suffocated. They immediately assumed that the solicitor had played a practical joke on them and rushing into the court gave a verdict against the gas company.

Sometimes, lawyers find it is kinder to avoid being too blunt in their pronouncements.

An accused and his solicitor were discussing the accused's chances. He had been caught red-handed.

'Do you think, Mr Comyn,' he asked, 'if I were to be convicted now, would I get a very long term?'

Dan Comyn thought for a moment before replying. 'No, Mick, I don't think so . . . no, I don't think so.'

He was telling the truth. In those days, the term between conviction and hanging was normally about three months.

In Monaghan town many years ago a butcher and a solicitor were very good friends, their respective places of work being on opposite sides of Church Square. The solicitor was partial to hunting and had a beautiful and distinctive red setter, of which the butcher was equally fond. The butcher was famous locally for the quality of his sausages. One morning, however, to his dismay he saw the setter disappearing from his shop with a string of sausages in his mouth.

Later that morning, he called on his friend.

'Good morning, Joe,' said the solicitor, 'to what do I owe the honour?'

'Well, I have a little problem.'

'Yes?'

'If a man's dog were to come into my shop and steal some sausages, would I be able to look to the owner for compensation?'

'Of course you would, of course you would. You can't have that sort of thing. People must keep their animals under control. Can you prove that the dog stole sausages?'

'I can surely. I saw him with my own eyes.'

The solicitor was getting excited.

'And would you know who the owner was?'

'I do, Matt. I know him well.'

'Well, you just give me his name and I'll have a letter out to him this afternoon. We'll get the price of your sausages and costs for you, no bother.'

The butcher smiled.

'There's no need for a letter, Matt. It was your Goldie took the sausages this morning and ate them in front of the shop. Just pay me one and sixpence and we'll regard that matter as settled.'

Mr Lardner was not amused, but put his hand in his pocket and paid the butcher his money.

The butcher was very pleased with his stratagem and was not slow to tell other friends of how he had outwitted the man of law. However, he was not seen to smile in the shop next morning, when a letter arrived in a brown envelope and he read: 'To legal advice concerning the theft of foodstuff from the premises of the plaintiff. 2/6d. Prompt payment will oblige.'

One fair day in Monaghan a farmer, his wife and her favourite son visited a solicitor. The wife proceeded to dictate the man's will, giving herself a life-tenancy and the remainder to the son. The farmer never opened his mouth and signed obediently when the will had been drawn up.

That afternoon, he returned.

'The wife and the lad have gone home,' he said. 'I want to make another will.'

A new will was drawn up leaving the farm to another son and various legacies to other children, while guaranteeing the right of the widow to stay in the family home for her lifetime and to receive an income.

'Keep that will now,' he told the solicitor, 'and not a word about it. I'll have peace in my day at any rate.'

A County Cork farmer came in to give instructions for his will, and after a long discussion the solicitor said, 'That's all right. You leave it all to me.'

'God, I suppose I'd better', said the farmer, 'for one way or another, you'll probably get it anyway.'

A newly qualified solicitor was left in charge of the office while his father was away on holidays. When the father returned, they went through the progress that had been made—or not made—in various matters during the father's absence.

'And what about the Wilkinson will case?' the father asked.

'Oh that', replied the son, 'I settled that case. It's all over and done.'

The father shook his head sadly and said, 'Don't you realise that that case educated you? Given a chance, it would have educated your son too.'

A case was being heard in the County Court in Tralee. There was a large attendance of solicitors from all over County Kerry and the Munster Bar was there in force. The judge organised everything and set out how the case should proceed. It went well but lasted two days, which was unusual in the County Court.

There was one little solicitor in court who did not open his mouth for the two days.

At last, when everyone was worn out and every aspect of the case had been examined frontways, backways and sideways, the judge, with a sigh of satisfaction at a good job done, asked, more from politeness than for any other reason: 'Well, that's that. Has anyone anything to add?'

The little solicitor stood up.

'Your Honour, I have a preliminary objection to make to your Honour's jurisdiction.'

STRATAGEMS

The polite word is 'stratagems'. Lay persons would be excused for calling them tricks.

Long before the FBI was even thought of, there was in Dublin a charming semi-rural establishment known popularly as 'The Informer's House'. Crown witnesses were lodged there between the magisterial investigation and the full trial.

A famous nineteenth-century case was the Crossmolina conspiracy, where the main evidence against alleged murderers was the testimony of an informer who, after making his deposition, was whisked away to Dublin for his own protection and put up in a pleasant Dublin suburb. He was well fed and supplied with an ample quantity of Guinness, but found his new life rather dull.

He shook the constitution of the realm to its foundations by issuing an ultimatum: his mind would lapse into complete oblivion unless it was stimulated by female companionship. Persons of exalted rank from Church and State tried to reason with him, but without success.

The upshot was that a willing lady was supplied and the shameless pair were entertained in luxury as the guests of the Empire.

The law officers had not been told of this development. On the eve of the trial, however, the Attorney General, John Naish, and his second in command, Peter O'Brien, met for the usual consultation. On paper, the case presented no particular difficulties and O'Brien stretched himself on a sofa and went to sleep. He was awakened by a terrified Attorney General, who had just learned the scandalous facts, with the added horror that the defence had also discovered them.

In Ireland—as it is well-known—before the arrival of television, murder, arson and terrorism were regarded as trivial incidents of daily life, but saints and scholars were sent into hysterics at the mere mention of sexual impropriety. If it were known that the executive had pimped for the randy informer, no juror could be found who would not commit perjury in the interests of virtue.

Poor Naish was babbling a long time on this topic before Peter really awakened himself to the situation.

'Peter, Peter, what shall we do if all this comes out?'

'I know what I shall do,' said Peter.

The leader for the defence, John Roche, was a man who in those politically incorrect days was described as 'as near to an old lady as ever an old gentleman could be'. He conducted his cases in the best traditions of Victorian femininity. When he rose to cross-examine the informer, Naish was frozen stiff with apprehension, but Peter, who knew his man, was quite comfortable.

At last, Roche advanced on the vulnerable topic and the Attorney General collapsed. Peter jumped to his feet.

'One moment,' he said, 'I hope that my dear and learned friend will not take my interruption as implying the smallest doubt or forgetfulness of the great reputation or the thoughtfulness and chivalry that makes Mr Roche the beloved leader of this circuit. I wish only to remind him that at the Munster bar the reputation of no lady is besmirched without necessity.'

The old gentleman blushed violently, became incoherent and continued with his case without a single question concerning the government's 'lewd guest'.

Like Daniel O'Connell, John Philpot Curran has entered the realms of folklore. The following anecdote has all the elements of a folk-tale:

A farmer went to the fair with £100 but, being afraid that his pocket might be picked or that he would fall into bad company, left it for safe keeping with the landlord of the public house where he was lodging. When he asked for it next morning, the landlord denied all knowledge of it. The farmer had no witnesses. He went to Curran for help.

Curran said, 'Have patience, my friend. Speak to him civilly and tell him that you are now convinced that you left your money elsewhere. Then, later in the day, take a friend with you, lodge another £100 with him and come to me.'

The farmer did not think much of this advice. He saw his second £100 going the way of the first, but he trusted Curran and reluctantly did as he was told. He came back and reported what he had done and asked Curran, 'Now, what?'

'Go back to him now,' said Curran, 'take him aside on his own and tell him that you have a purchase to make and ask for your money back.'

Off went the farmer again and returned with his £100. He was somewhat relieved but pointed out to the counsellor that he was still no better off than when he came to consult Curran that morning.

But Curran had not finished.

'Now,' he advised, 'call your friend. Return with him to the landlord and ask for the £100 that your friend saw you leave with him.'

Back he went and the landlord handed over the money.

———————

A priest brought an action against Lord Doneraile at Cork Assizes in the late eighteenth century. Curran had to examine Mr St Leger, Lord Doneraile's brother, and in order to reduce the effect of his evidence described him in gross and insulting language, but did not actually mention him by name.

When St Leger came to the table and took up the testament to swear, Curran suddenly spoke to him in an apparently concerned and respectful tone: 'Oh, Mr St

Leger, the jury will, I am sure, believe you without the ceremony of swearing an oath. Your character will justify us from insisting on your oath.'

Taken in by Curran's sudden docility, St Leger was, at the same time, too distracted by his irritation at the earlier attack to spot what Curran was up to.

'Sir,' he smirked, 'I am glad you have changed the opinion that you had of me when you described me a while ago.'

Click. The trap was sprung.

'What, sir, you confess it was a description of yourself. Gentlemen, act as you please, but I leave it to you to say whether a thousand oaths could bind the conscience of the man I have just described.'

A duel followed . . . naturally!

John Philpot Curran had a younger brother who was an attorney—very like him, but taller and better looking. He had a good deal of his brother's humour, a little wit, and much satire, but his slang was infinite and his conduct very dissolute. He was, in fact, what may be termed the best blackguard of his profession and that was saying a great deal for him. Curran had justly excluded him from his house, but occasionally relieved his finances until these demands became so importunate that at length he had to call a halt.

'Sir', said the attorney to Jonah Barrington one day, 'if you will speak to my brother, I am sure he'll give me something handsome before the week is out!'

Barrington assured him that he was mistaken but the brother's reply was a loud laugh.

There was a small space of dead wall at that time directly facing Curran's house in Ely Place, against which the brother procured a written permission to build a little wooden box. He accordingly got a carpenter, one of his comrades, to erect a cobbler's stall there for him; and dressing up in the appropriate clothes he wrote over his stall: 'Curran, Cobbler. Shoes toe-pieced, soled or heeled on the shortest notice. When the stall is shut, inquire over the way.'

Curran, on returning from court, saw his brother hard at work, with a crowd of sedan chair carriers lounging around him.

The attorney just nodded to his brother, cried 'How do you do, Jack?' and went on with his cobbling.

Curran rushed inside and sent out a servant with money for the brother. The show-board was taken down, the stall removed and the attorney promised never to set up as a cobbler again.

———

Normally, when one person does some work for another there is a contract, written or oral, as to the work to be done and the amount to be paid. In certain cases, where there is no clear agreement but one person has actually carried out some work for another, the former is entitled to be compensated for the amount that he or she has earned. This is known as quantum meruit.

Two barristers were driving in a hired car to the judge's lodgings in Athlone for dinner. The car broke down and another had to be procured. The first barrister was famous for his meanness. At the dinner, a member of the circuit asked if he had paid anything to the driver of the car that had broken down.

Paddy goggled at him, his face aglow with a triumphant smile.

'I nearly did,' he confessed, 'but den I remembered that it was an entire contract, and dat he couldn't plead *quantum meruit.*'

———

Daniel O'Connell was never above trickery if it achieved his object.

He was defending in a murder case and the most damning evidence against his client was a hat which had been found at the scene of the crime and had been positively identified by a prosecution witness.

O'Connell was called to cross-examine. He stood up, picked up the hat and examined it carefully while everyone in the court-room watched him. He turned it this way and that and finally came to the inner rim. He turned it to the light and began to spell out the letters of a name. 'J.A.M.E.S. F.O.G.A.R.T.Y.' This was the accused's name.

'Was this name,' he asked the witness, 'written inside the hat when you found it?'

'It was so.'

'Did you see it there?'

'I did so.'

'You didn't write it yourself.'

'I did not. It was written like that when I found it.'

'And this is the hat that you found?'

'It is surely.'

'My Lord,' O'Connell addressed the bench, 'there is an end to the case. There is no name whatever inscribed in the hat.'

On another occasion, O'Connell had a hopeless murder case before a new and inexperienced judge. He deliberately put leading questions to one of his witnesses. When the judge properly disallowed them, O'Connell put on an appearance of outrage and gathered up his papers.

'Very well, since you refuse me permission to defend my client, my Lord, I leave his fate to your hands, his blood be upon your head if he is condemned.'

He left the court and the terrified judge later instructed the jury to acquit.

But even O'Connell was not proof against stratagems.

He once appeared as complainant alleging that a Dublin attorney named Toby Glasscock had threatened to send a servant to horse-whip him. Since it was beneath

O'Connell's dignity to fight a duel with Glasscock, he was applying to have him bound over to keep the peace.

Glasscock replied that a big man like O'Connell should not have been frightened of any breach of the peace from a little person like his servant. He offered to produce the servant in court. When the court agreed, he reached under the table, brought up a bag, placed it on the table, opened it and lifted out a tiny black child, clothed in green livery.

'Here is the horse-whipper.'

For once, O'Connell was laughed out of court.

Judge Martin Connolly was the martinet of judges. Patrick Lindsay was scared stiff on the day of his first appearance before him.

Seamus Henchy was first in the ring. He was KO'd ruthlessly.

Next came John Willie O'Connor. He was knocked through the ropes.

Third was Conor Maguire. Two black eyes, a smashed jaw and a ruptured spleen.

Finally, Lindsay came on. Connolly sized him up as if deciding which blow would cause most damage with least effort.

'Are your proofs in order?'

'Yes, my Lord, subject to your searching scrutiny.'

A killer tired of easy game, Connolly nodded.

'As long as you know that.'

Lindsay sailed through the following fortnight.

A Dutch smuggler of lace, perfume, good old brandy and expensive cigars into Munster was the owner in the last century of half a dozen craft, mostly ketches which were registered in foreign parts. They did not cost him very much originally and when they were caught and condemned, he used to repurchase them at auction at a nominal price.

With time, his boats became too well-known for comfort and detentions and captures became difficult to avoid. Risks had to be taken and the business was losing money. At length, the Dutchman had an idea. He had been content to allow his ships, when captured, to be condemned without more ado, but he began to think that if he resisted the condemnation and compelled the Crown to proceed according to law, he could make condemnation such a nuisance and expense that His Majesty's navy might be instructed to turn a blind eye on his ships in the future.

Accordingly, he entered an appearance and contested the right of the Crown to condemn as prize one of his old ketches.

The naval personnel, who were concerned with the detection and capture of his boat, had to be collected and brought to Cork. By this time, they were scattered all over the globe, thousands of miles apart. Even for those who were in closer waters, the Second Sea Lord's department had the trouble and annoyance of the sorting out of different ships, of members of the crew travelling to Ireland and sitting in court for days waiting for the case to come on.

When it did come on finally, the law officers were no sailors and had no practical knowledge of navigation. It turned out to be very hard for the Crown to prove the exact spot at which the sailing vessel was located the first time it was observed, when a sloop moving at 15 m.p.h. had perceived it eight miles distant, on a recorded bearing, and overhauled it only after a chase of one hour and five minutes.

At the end of the day, the ship was, of course, condemned and the smuggler duly bought her back for £40.

It had cost His Majesty the King over £2,000 pounds to earn that £40.

———

There once appeared before a jury a man who was suing his brother-in-law for the price of three hundred pairs of boots. Both parties were prosperous traders in a country town, rivals in as much as both dealt in boots and shoes, but they obliged one other by selling each other stock at cost price if required. They had quarrelled over politics at a time when the last hundred pairs of boots sent across by the plaintiff had not been paid for. It appeared to be a perfectly plain case.

Unfortunately, it was tried before Mr Justice Johnson before whom no case could remain plain for ten minutes, and the defendant, Mick McCarthy, was allowed—most improperly—to spring upon the court an undreamt-of story. He said that he had never bought boots from the plaintiff, Jimmy Hanley, or from anybody else, that his warehouse and all its contents were in fact the property of the plaintiff and run in the defendant's name as a trade dodge. He, McCarthy, was no more than a hired drudge.

This farrago of nonsense commended itself to Johnson as inspired revelation; so far as he was able, he presented it to the jury as hallowed truth. He did not allude to the absurdity of an employer suing his servant for the price of goods when he needed no litigation to put into his hands all that the servant possessed. The jury agreed with the judge that the defendant was not a purchaser but only a hireling.

'Can we appeal that, counsellor?' Hanley asked when the case was over.

'Why should you?'

'Sure, of course, I'll appeal it. 'Tis all nonsense.'

'What is the value of the boots the fellow has in his store?'

'Sure, he have a thousand pounds worth of boots, but what use are they to me? I'm bate.'

'Oh, I don't know about that,' said counsel. 'They are now yours.'

He made some suggestions based on a famous case involving the Duchess of Kingston.

'But, Counsellor, I can't get beyond Cork tonight.'

'By train, no. But are there no horses?'

When the two parties reached Cork at half-past eleven that night, the winners went out to celebrate. Hanley said in McCarthy's hearing that he was tired and was off to bed.

Next morning McCarthy and his supporters set out for home. They buttonholed every friend and acquaintance on the way and related with appropriate guffaws how they had fooled the judge, the jury and the brother-in-law. When McCarthy reached his shop, however, he found the shutters were still on the windows and the door was open. He rushed in and turned on the light. His great emporium was empty! There was not a boot in it. Hanley had them all.

McCarthy now launched an action himself. He would not negotiate. He despised offers of honest adjustment. He claimed to get his boots back. Of course, he had to commence by explaining that on the previous occasion he had committed wilful and corrupt perjury. That did not trouble him. By the custom of the country he was entitled to do so without a stain on his character. When he described the events that followed his victory celebration, the judge laughed heartily and then held for the defendant.

It was the ghost of the Duchess of Kingston who had risen up against McCarthy. Following the precedent established by her case, the verdict of the first jury had made Hanley the owner of the boots by estoppel of record.

WILLS

A gentleman lay dying in a country house in County Roscommon. He told his housekeeper to send for the priest. She did so and the priest went in to the old man and spent some time with him. Then he asked for a table and candles and administered Extreme Unction. The old man asked for pen, ink and paper. When the housekeeper brought them, he told her to leave the room. Shortly afterwards, he rang a bell and called for the servant girl. She was sent up. When she came down again, the housekeeper asked her eagerly what she had been doing up there.

'They made me sign something.'

'What was it?'

'I don't know, Mrs Doherty, some sort of paper that Fr Flynn had written out. The master had signed it before me.'

That night the old man died and, before he was cold, the housekeeper ransacked his bedroom and found, as she had expected, his will. He had left her the house and a considerable sum of money. The will was signed by the priest and the servant girl. She had never expected so much and was, at first, delighted. Then she got frightened. Maybe it wasn't enough to have those two signatures. That Molly Fogarty was an ignorant girl. The lawyers might not think much of her signature. It needed someone as good as the priest to sign it. She took the will downstairs, got out the pen and ink, added her own signature to the document and put it back in the drawer. Her inheritance was now safe.

Her high hopes collapsed, however, when the will was proven and she learned that a witness to a will cannot inherit under it.

———

A judge on the King's Bench whose elevation was due as usual to his political affiliations rather than to his knowledge of the law announced in the course of a will case that he thought it very clear that the testator intended to keep a life interest in the estate to himself.

At first, the bar managed not to laugh outright but lost control when John Philpot Curran commented: 'Very true, my Lord, very true! Testators generally do secure life-interests to themselves. But in this case I rather think your Lordship takes the *will* for the *deed*.'

———

Good intentions can often lead to hard cases, bad law and scant justice.

Upstairs in a country farmhouse, the master lay dying. He had received the last sacraments and, having no near relatives, was left to the care of a servant girl. Downstairs, his friends were drinking his whiskey, when someone suggested that the dying man might want to make a will and a messenger was sent into the nearest town to bring back the first solicitor he could find.

The only solicitor available was a man who was known to be more than a little 'touched'. The servant girl took him up to the sick man's bedroom but then lingered outside the door until she heard the good news that her master was leaving her a modest legacy. The will was properly executed and the solicitor departed into the night.

More drink was consumed downstairs and an interesting discussion arose as to whether in point of law a lunatic could draw up and witness the will of a sane man. There was no question about the sanity of the man upstairs, but the more empty bottles piled up, the more the jurisprudential amateurs in the kitchen wondered whether his will might be invalidated by the testamentary incapacity of the solicitor who had drawn it.

This troubled the girl and she pressed them on it until they decided that it might be safer to send for a second solicitor. The messenger was dispatched and came back with another man, who drew up another will, one of the guests having explained to the patient that the first will was legally invalid for the reason mentioned. Again the girl listened at the door but to her consternation this time the testator forgot her legacy.

She slipped on her shawl and walked all the way into town to the office of the first solicitor.

'Mr O'Toole', she said, 'is it true law that any will drawn up by you would be set aside by a court because you are mad?'

'Who said that?' exploded Mr O'Toole.

She told him the whole story.

The sequel was sad. O'Toole only had time to issue writs against his slanderers before he was locked in the local asylum. The girl's efforts to prove the first will were thrown out.

No small farmer in Munster ever dreamed of himself as the absolute owner of his land. It was there to provide for the family. If death called before the farm had been passed on in marriage bargain, he had to provide in his will that in due course one of his own name should be master of the place. If he had a son, there was no problem. If he had no children, he left it to his widow during widowhood, then to a nephew of his name. If he had daughters only, there were difficulties ahead.

The great preoccupation of the dying man was to beware of his own widow, if she had no children, or if she was young. Care had to be taken to give her no title that would pass to a new family. In spite of this, she would be besieged by suitors, enterprising young fellows who would take small wages in the hope that once they got a foothold in the farm, they would manage somehow, some day, to own it.

The Catch 22 was that a widow who had possession, as trustee for her children or her late husband's relatives, could not hope to get a fortune if she married, so had to marry for love. In spite or because of this, there was a tendency on the part of widow trustees to select good-looking young men, regardless of social rank.

Once married, the pair would set to work to acquire the farm to the exclusion of the children or the relatives. In the old days the rent would be allowed to run into arrears, the widow would be evicted and the new husband would then take it. The equity side of the County Court eventually put an end to this by declaring that the new tenancy was still held in trust. The next trick was to arrange that a collusive friend would take the new tenancy but, where land is concerned, friends are not always reliable, and the friend was frequently tempted to grab the land for himself.

WITNESS BITES BACK

Barristers are trained to hunt and to kill. It gives a certain satisfaction, therefore, when the hare turns and savages the hound.

A boy was accused of stealing a calf and Daniel O'Connell was cross-examining the wife of the calf's owner. Irrelevantly he asked her how she had come by the calf, calling her patronisingly his 'good woman'.

'What's that to you?', was her sullen reply.

'Oh, I have a reason for asking.'

'Honestly then, which is more than the boy who took it can say.'

'Oh, of course, you wouldn't have it any other way, but how did you get the calf?'

'To buy it, I did.'

'Where did you get the money?'

She was not going to give away this secret and he kept badgering her until she burst out, 'Ah, you knows all the *roguery* of it, but you don't know the *honesty* of it!'

An honest character witness was asked by the judge concerning the accused, 'Would he be the kind of man to steal money?'

The witness thought for a moment and asked, 'How much?'

A solicitor was appearing in a District Court to defend a man who had been charged with stealing a turkey. The person who claimed to be the owner of the turkey was a formidable woman from the Midlands, well able to stand up to cross-examination and give as good as she got.

The solicitor opted for a challenge to the identity of the turkey found in the possession of his client. One turkey looks very like another turkey. How could she possibly tell that this particular turkey was her missing bird.

'Ho ho,' she laughed, 'wouldn't I be a foolish woman now not to know one of me own birds?'

'But what was there about it that you recognised? Can you tell us anything that made it different from other birds?'

'Sure, everything was different. The feathers was different. Wasn't there feathers missing from the tail?'

'I don't know,' said the solicitor. 'Are you seriously asking the court to believe that you could tell a bird by a few missing feathers? Have you no better way of knowing it?'

'Well, I had, sir. Sure, I knew it well by the balls of it. Oh, I'd know its balls anywhere.'

This was the opening the solicitor had been waiting for.

'Hold on, ma'am, hold on. Let's stop there. Did you or did you not say when this case began that you had a hen turkey stolen from you?'

'I did, indeed, and I had. By that fellow there.'

'Then how could you possibly recognise its balls.'

'Well, God in heaven, the tongue of you! I knew her by the terrible racket she made, the bawls she would let out of her.'

A smarmy Serjeant at Law stayed in a newly opened hotel in Kerry. The wife of the proprietor was describing to him the splendours of her establishment.

Finally, the Serjeant interrupted, 'So you live in this earthly paradise? A regular garden of Eden. Tell me, have you any serpent here?'

'No, Serjeant,' was her reply, 'but we'd always be happy to have you back!'

A little girl from Cork had been knocked down while crossing the road. Because of her young age the question of whether she might or might not understand the nature and meaning of the oath caused flutterings in the court until the judge intervened and asked her in a kindly manner, 'What happens, Mary Anne, if you tell a lie on the Bible?'

'You goes to Hell.'

That was enough for everybody and she was duly sworn.

The examination in chief began.

'Mary Anne, do you live near McCurtin Road?'

'He blew no horr-an,' she replied.

'No, Mary Anne, we have not come to that yet. Tell the judge where you live.'

'He blew no horr-an.'

'Did you see a car coming over the hill?'

'He blew no horr-an.'

This went on until the judge stopped the case. The girl's barrister avoided the judge's eye by looking intently at his solicitor who appeared to be momentarily hypnotised by the toes of his shoes.

Maurice Healy, the author of The Old Munster Circuit, *describes the differences between Irish and English witnesses:*

The Englishman goes into a court of law unwillingly, fearfully, and especially apprehensive of cross-examination. No doubt there are occasional witnesses of that kind in Ireland, too; but the vast majority go to give their evidence as a cricketer walks to the wicket. Each is confident that he will not be bowled until he has knocked up a good score; each is disappointed if the bowler limits his efforts to preventing the score from rising, and does not attack his wicket.

In the late Edward Marjoribanks' *Life of Carson* he cites a number of incidences of English witnesses being bowled over by a cross-examination, deadly in England, but which would not have knocked a feather off a Kerryman. Instead of the awkward silence chronicled in the biography, there would have been an indignant repetition of the question, followed by an immediate turn towards the judge, who would be swamped in a deluge of irrelevant matter, as though it were a complete explanation of the problem under examination, and by the time the witness would be brought back to the point he would have thought of a plausible answer to the actual question he had been asked.

———————

A man accused of theft was told to hold up his right hand to swear. He held up his left hand. The clerk, naturally suspicious, scolded him.

'Hold up your right hand.'

The accused still held up his left hand.

'I told you to hold up your right hand.'

He still kept his left hand in the air.

'Now, listen here, are you deaf or what? I'm telling you to hold up your right hand, your right hand.'

With the innocence of a new-born babe, the prisoner appealed to the judge.

'May it please your Honour, I'm left-handed.'

———————

A prosecuting counsel was examining an eye-witness to the shooting of a landlord. The witness's deposition had described the shooting clearly, but in court he hummed and hawed and his mind had apparently gone blank.

Counsel knew very well why he was not forthcoming and, in the best public school manner, decided to shame him into telling the truth.

'Are you not ashamed of yourself to be such a coward?'

The witness had not been to a public school.

'Isn't it better to be a coward for five minutes, than dead all the rest of your life?'

A man was killed during a fight at a fair. The medical witness demonstrated how death had occurred. He explained that the skull was like an eggshell and, if you hit it with a shillelagh, it would be just like hitting an egg with a spoon. He mimed the tapping of a spoon on an egg and the cracking of the shell.

At a later stage of the trial, prosecuting counsel was cross-examining one of the defence witnesses, who claimed that there had been nothing more than the ordinary hurly-burly, that a few blows might have been exchanged but no one had used any undue violence and he had seen nothing out of the ordinary.

'Come now,' said the barrister, 'you have heard the medical witness. This unfortunate poor man's head was smashed like an eggshell.'

'So you say,' replied the witness, 'but you just tell me what business had a man with a skull like an eggshell at the fair of Cappawhite?'

A suitor in a long-drawn-out case in Lord Norbury's court, a man called Toby M'Cormick was driven mad by the final loss of his suit. He not only spent his days hanging around the court but got it into his head that he was Lord Norbury and that Norbury was Toby M'Cormick. At the end of Lord Norbury's charges he would cry out, mimicking the judge perfectly, 'Find for the plaintiff.'

This always raised a great laugh at the judge's expense, particularly since it was done so innocently. Every time it happened, the judge seemed to be taken by surprise and turning to Peter Jackson would bellow, 'Jackson, turn Toby M'Cormick out of court!'

And everyone bellowed again, half expecting to see Jackson turn the judge himself out.

———

A dispute arose in relation to a will. An old man disinherited his relatives and left everything to an ancient neighbour who had looked after him in his final years. The relatives contested the will on the grounds that the deceased had not been of sound mind, memory and understanding when he made his will. It was the job of counsel to show that this was the case.

He examined the sole beneficiary and tried to make him admit that the old man's behaviour was, to say the least of it, odd. The neighbour, naturally, would not accept any such thing. In his view, the testator's mind was clear as a bell.

'Clear as a bell,' said counsel. 'And yet he had the habit of soliloquising?'

'He what?'

'He was known to soliloquise.'

The old witness shook his head in bemused incomprehension.

The judge asked counsel to explain the long word that he was using.

'Soliloquising means talking to himself when he was alone.'

'Oh, is that it? I have you now,' said the witness.

'Well, didn't he, didn't he often talk to himself when he was alone?'

'Alone, is it?'

'Yes, didn't he talk to himself when he was alone?'

The witness looked at counsel as benevolently as if he were correcting a foolish child.

'God bless you, sir, I was never with him when he was alone.'

———

At the end of the nineteenth century, there was a rabies scare in Ireland. Local authorities were ordered to destroy all cattle suffering or suspected of suffering from the disease. If it could be proved that the animal had rabies, no compensation was payable to the owner but, if there was only suspicion, the owner had to be paid the value of the beast. Here was the rub. A number of experts came up with a theory that the only way to establish beyond doubt that a cow had rabies was by microscopic examination of the spinal cord and, since that could not be carried out while the animal was alive, she was necessarily slaughtered on suspicion which might or might not be verified later. The local authorities ended up paying for cattle which, in fact, turned out to be rabid.

One local council decided to challenge the experts and produced in the witness box an ancient 'cow-doctor' whose testimony was to shatter medical science. He was not quite sober, but that was rarely noticed in Judge Adams's court.

'The cow had rabies and before she died I proved it,' he claimed.

'How did you prove it?'

'By d'infallible test.'

'Did you examine her spinal cord while she was still alive?'

'I did not, but I brought a dog into de byre where she was in her stall and de cow barked. Dat's d'infallible test.'

'Was that the only test?'

'No. In dis case dere was another infallible test.'

'What was it?'

'Dere was the sudden death of d'cow.'

'Describe what happened. Did she die very suddenly.'

'Suddenly surely. I shot her.'

During the trial of a smuggler in Cork, the prosecuting Attorney General was Mr Richard Cherry, the author of an unrivalled textbook on landlord and tenant, an expert on the rental value of irreclaimable bog, but no sailor. He also lacked any vestige of a sense of humour.

He called the petty officer who had boarded the captured

ketch. The latter testified that the ship's manifest revealed a cargo of onions which were nowhere to be found and that the ship's clearance was from Rotterdam to Iceland and it had been captured about eleven miles south-south-west of the Stags off the coast of County Cork.

Cherry ponderously asked the petty officer: 'Assuming that this ship was carrying a cargo of onions from Rotterdam to Iceland, in your opinion, at the time of capture, was she off her course?'

For a moment, the petty officer was speechless. Then he leant over the rail of the witness-box, pushed his chin as far as he could in the direction of the Attorney General and shouted: 'Off 'is course? Off 'is bloody course? Why, I should bloody well think 'e was off his course. The bleeder should 'ave been somewhere off the east coast of England.'

In the days when money was money, Lord Clancarty, who was fond of a drop, was charged with various fraudulent practices. The prosecutor opened up to the jury some of the counts of the indictment and wound up by saying: 'But there is one count to which there can be no possible defence. It will be proved that the accused obtained credit at the Royal Hibernian Hotel to the extent of over £150 without disclosing that he was in fact an undischarged bankrupt, and that is a criminal offence.'

'I have been looking at the bill,' said the judge, who had a sense of humour, 'and, of course, counsel for the accused will say that there was implied disclosure. I see that the bill for the first week is £49 1s. 3d. and I have been checking the items. Counsel will no doubt say that no one except an undischarged bankrupt could afford to incur such a bill in such a time.'

During the course of his bankruptcy proceedings, Clancarty, after giving a most complicated account of the disappearance of a very expensive item of jewellery, was told by counsel that he had committed wilful and corrupt perjury.

Although habitually tipsy, Clancarty prided himself upon behaving like a gentleman on all occasions. He swayed gracefully in the box and replied, 'I am not quite sure that I apprehend the question, Mr O'Riordan, but I will take your word for it.'

When one reads about the aristocracy and magistracy of Wexford in the late eighteenth century, one gets a better understanding of the causes of 1798. The following anecdote shows them at their most typical:

A handsome young woman was maidservant to a Mrs Lett, who was considered to be a great patriot/rebel. One evening, the girl was sitting at her mistress's window singing songs to airs that were not considered orthodox by the aristocracy.

The Marquis of Ely, the High Sheriff and other gentlemen of the county, were retiring after their wine from the grand jury, and heard the young girl singing. Since the song sounded to their loyal ears as of a rebellious tendency, it was thought advisable to demolish the fragile parts of Mrs Lett's house without delay. Accordingly, the Marquis, the High Sheriff and their friends, to preserve the peace and protect the consititution from such treacherous maid-servants, started to hurl stones at the singer, smashed all the windows to the benefit of the local glazier and almost put fees into the pockets not only of the surgeon but of the sexton and coroner also.

In spite of their rank and offices, they were indicted and Jonah Barrington was briefed to defend his Lordship. He did his utmost to make the worse appear the better cause, but the marquis felt that he was being too delicate in his handling of the maidservant and asked for permission to ask her a few questions himself. Permission was granted.

'Now, girl,' said the marquis, 'by the oath you have taken, did you not say you would split my skull open?'

'Why, then, by the virtue of my oath,' said the girl, turning to the judge, 'it would not be worth my while to split his skull open, my Lord.'

'Ha! ha!' said the marquis, 'now I have her,' assuming that she had referred to payment by his enemies for killing him.

'And why, girl, would it not be worth your while?'

'Because, my Lord if I had split your Lordship's skull open, by virtue of my oath, I am sure and certain I should have found little or nothing inside of it!'

Whereas before Independence, criminal cases had been titled Rex (or Regina) v. John Doe, *after 1921 this became* The State v. John Doe.

In Cork in the early nineteen twenties, an old lag heard the clerk call out, 'The State against Finbar O' Sullivan'.

'Jaysus, I'm outnumbered!' he exclaimed.

A prosecutor was cross-examining a witness in Carrickmacross. He sailed near the wind asking for an opinion from the witness about a well-known smuggler.

'What sort of fellow would you say he was, Mr Bannigan?

Packy looked at him thoughtfully, as if he had been asked a very hard question. He screwed up his features and then let his breath out in a puff before explaining confidentially, 'Well, I'll tell you this, sir, he was the sort of fellow that you wouldn't know what sort of fellow he was!'

A solicitor was ordered by his doctor to go abroad for a year. He left his practice in the hands of a young cousin and his managing clerk, Patsy. He also left a long list of written instructions.

After dealing with current cases, regular clients and other matters, the final sentence read: 'Whatever you do, don't sack Patsy. He'll rob you, but he'll see that nobody else does.'

A young process-server returned from his first mission without having served his writ. He was asked what had happened, had he not found the place.

'Oh, I found the place all right. A maid opened the door. I asked her if her master was in and she said to me, "The misthress is the masther here, and she's out."'

A wife, who had alleged cruelty, had been a difficult client from the very start. She had made the solicitor's life miserable. She had tormented her barrister. In court, she was an impossible witness, straying into hearsay at every possible opportunity, bad-mouthing the solicitor and contradicting her counsel.

In the end, he was forced into a leading question.

'So your husband attempted to strangle you, did he?'

'He did, surely.'

The temptation was too great.

'Well, why, in Heaven's name, didn't he succeed?'

Tim Healy was cross-examining an old lady from the Coombe and began, 'Now then, Mary Anne . . .'

Without hesitation, she snapped, 'Mrs Hagerty, to you, Tim!'

A witness at Kilkenny Assizes was asked if, when examined before the magistrate, the account that he had given of a certain transaction was not materially different from the story that he was telling now. He admitted quite freely that this was true but said that he had been humbugged in the business. Counsel, who was not the brightest, exclaimed, 'Humbugged? What is that? I don't understand what you mean?'

'Don't you, sir,' said the witness, ' well then, I'll just have to explain it in your own way by putting a case. Suppose now I should tell his Lordship here and the gentlemen of the jury that you were an able counsel and they were to believe me, every man's son of them would be humbugged, my dear, that's all!'

———————

Percy French was sued for libel for his song about the West Clare Railway company. He arrived late for the trial and when asked by the judge why he was late, explained that he had come by the West Clare railway.

———————

Once at Dublin's Quarter Sessions there was a chairman who was so lenient to women accused that they almost invariably got off.

One day, he was not there and another justice was presiding. A Dublin woman was indicted for uttering forged bank notes.

According to the usual form of the law, the Clerk of the Crown asked her if she was ready to take her trial.

'I am not', said she. 'I'll be tried by the other judge or not at all.'

The chairman tried to explain to her the impossiblity of this.

'He can't try you,' he said.

'Can't try me? Didn't he try me twice before!'

———————

A browbeating counsel was examining a witness about the distance from one point to another in a certain place.

'Four yards, two feet and six inches,' was the instant reply.

'And how can you be so exact, my friend?'

'Because I expected that some fool or other would ask me about it, so I measured it.'

———————

ACKNOWLEDGMENTS

This book owes its inspiration to many frequently visited sources, which themselves have never ceased to draw on one another down the ages in an intricate pattern, legal raconteurs and their audiences having always been traditionalists who do not relish novelty but rejoice in the warmth of the familiar. These yarn-spinners, in the seventeenth century or the twentieth, like the ancient Irish bard loved 'the sprigs with their woven tops tied with a hundred knots, after the manner of the Celts, which the artists employed about their mysteries'.

Most prominent among this jurisprudential heritage has been *Sgéalaigheacht Chéitinn*, stories from Geoffrey Keating's *History of Ireland* (An Iodh Morainn), Sir Jonah Barrington's *Personal Recollections*, Richard Lalor Sheil's *Legal and Political Sketches*, John Mitchel's *Jail Journal*, various retellings of the exploits of Daniel O'Connell, A.M. Sullivan's memoirs *The Last of the Serjeants*, H. Montgomery Hyde's life of *Edward Carson*, *Lord Morris and Killanin's* biography by his daughter, V.T.H. Delaney's life of *Christopher Palles, Lord Chief Baron of Her Majesty's Court of Exchequer in Ireland*, Burke's *Old Western Circuit*, Maurice Healy's eternal *Old Munster Circuit*, James Comyn's many tales of his uncle, Michael Comyn, Patrick MacKenzie's *Lawful Occasions: The Old Eastern Circuit* and Patrick Lindsay's *Memories*.

I thank them all for opening the back of the wardrobe and enabling me to wander so happily through Narnia.